COMMUNIST COUNCILMAN

FROM HARLEM

COMMUNIST COUNCILMAN FROM HARLEM

Autobiographical Notes
Written in a Federal Penitentiary

by BENJAMIN J. DAVIS

INTERNATIONAL PUBLISHERS
New York

Library of Congress Catalog Card Number: 69-17615
Manufactured in the United States of America

CONTENTS

APPENDIX

FOREWORD

This book tells the story of a Southern black man who became a Communist in the struggle to save a black youth from electrocution in Georgia. The youth was Angelo Herndon, a young Communist who was seeking to unite black and white unemployed workers in the fight for jobs and bread in Atlanta during the height of the Great Depression of the 1930s. The author of this book was his lawyer.

In later years the author was a frontline fighter against racism and political corruption in New York City. The first black Communist to be elected to legislative office in the United States, he was a City Councilman for six years, from 1944 through 1949. Most of his votes came from Harlem's black people, but he could not have won without the support of thousands of progressive white voters.

Benjamin J. Davis's story is an inspiration in the struggle for black liberation and socialism. That is why the Department of Justice kept his book in prison for ten years after the author himself was released.

The writing was done under enormous difficulties in a tiny, poorly lighted cell in the jim-crow section of the Federal Penitentiary at Terre Haute, Indiana, several months of it in solitary confinement. The author was placed in solitary when he filed suit in the courts to end racial segregation in Federal prisons. He was allowed out of his dungeon only ten minutes a week. His food was often cold when it reached him. When I read this book, I am reminded of Julius Fucik, the Czech Communist, who wrote his immortal *Notes From the Gallows* in a Nazi death cell.

Ben, as everyone called him, was my dear comrade. He was framed with me and nine other Communist leaders, as many black men and many Communists were framed before. We were jailed under the infamous Smith Act, drafted by Rep. Howard Smith of Alexandria, Virginia, a notorious racist. This fascist,

thought-control law was called into full service early in the
Cold War. After serving a five-year term, my dear friend was
released in 1955, but his manuscript remained in prison. Ben's
wife, Nina, disregarding all rebuffs, and with the help of John
J. Abt, Ben's attorney, kept up the pressure on the Bureau of
Prisons until the key turned in the lock, and the manuscript was
surrendered to her in 1965—one year after her husband died.

Ben Davis was a modest man. He was the central figure in
dramatic battles on both sides of the Mason and Dixon line. But
he gives all credit to the Communist Party and to the black people and other brave fighters, and none to himself. We see this,
for example, in a stirring Atlanta scene. As he left the courthouse
during the Herndon trial, the Kluxers surrounded him and
threatened him with death. In the nick of time a group of black
men, led by a brave preacher, surrounded Ben. They came prepared for action. The cowardly terrorists melted away. His courageous friends, not himself, are the heroes in Ben's eyes.

Ben never took the easy way out. He met the enemy head on
from the day he came to Herndon's defense. Marx and Engels
tell us in the *Communist Manifesto* that, "The history of all
hitherto existing society is the history of class struggles." It can
truly be said that the history of Ben's people is the history of
constant struggle against oppressors. Ben felt this almost from
childhood, and later he came to understand also how the struggle for black liberation was related to the class struggle and
socialism.

His own family was a link to ten generations of chattel slavery,
when the bondsmen rose again and again against their masters.
Ben's grandfather fought back when Ben's grandmother was
flogged savagely. The grandfather himself was then beaten almost
to death. Older members of the Davis family also remembered
the few years of political democracy in the Reconstruction period
after the Civil War. Then, black men sat in the U.S. Senate and
Congress. Black and white legislators enacted progressive laws
in Mississippi, Alabama, Georgia, South Carolina and other
Southern states. Black and white troops curbed the Ku Klux Klan.

After the short-lived revolutionary period of Reconstruction, democracy was blotted out in the South when the black people were surrendered to the racist terrorists by President Hayes in the Great Betrayal of 1877. Night fell on the Georgia town where the Davis family lived, and on black people throughout the South. Slavery turned to peonage; the vote was taken away; all civil rights vanished. Freedom-loving black men and women were hanged or burned to death by the mobs of the landowners and their hangers-on. By the time Ben was born on September 8, 1903, disfranchisement of black people was written into new state constitutions and laws throughout the South.

Black people found new ways to press for freedom. They came together in their churches and fraternal societies, and new leaders arose. One of these was Benjamin Davis, Sr., who became the leading spokesman of Georgia's black people.

This book sheds much light on Negro history in a dramatic and personal way. Ben points out that father and son represented two very different stages in the black people's fight for freedom. They had different struggle tactics and different ultimate goals. The father risked his life to win reforms for his people. But he saw these reforms as ends in themselves. He had the illusion that the rising white capitalists would help him win civil rights from the white landlords of the Old South.

Ben gives full credit to his father's courage and devotion to the struggle. He fearlessly crusaded for the vote for his disfranchised people. His home was a sort of Underground Railway station for sharecroppers fleeing from debt and lynching. The racists hated him. Ku Klux Klan crosses burned on his lawn from time to time. But he treated the racists' warnings with contempt. "The worst thing you can do is to run away from them," he told Ben. And he continued with his work.

The elder Davis was a national figure. Dr. W. E. B. Du Bois, the great black historian, speaks of him with deep respect in the second volume of his trilogy, *The Black Flame*. He grew up in utmost poverty in the little cotton-picking town of Dawson, which the son describes so vividly in this book. The town still "reeked with the stench of the slave market," when Ben Jr. grew up there. "The Negro side of the tracks," he says, "was like the slave hovels of 1860." But Ben's father, a talented and vigorous man, rose rapidly. He won political leadership through a black fraternal society. He became the publisher and editor of the *Independent*, an influential newspaper. He advanced in the Republican Party and was the GOP's national committee member from Georgia for some years.

His success, however, did not save him from the indignities inflicted on all black people in the South. When he entered a bus in Atlanta he was treated like the poorest sharecropper, and compelled to take a seat in the back. Nor could he use the washroom in the bus station if the word "Colored" was not on the door.

Ben's father looked on the GOP as the party of Abraham Lincoln, the Great Emancipator, as many black people did then. He finally lost these illusions when he found that the Republicans were betraying his people. At the end of his life his sympathy for the party his son had chosen was rising.

In contrast to his father, Ben was a revolutionary from early manhood. Ben soon came to understand that black liberation is tied to the victory of working class power and can be assured only by socialism. He knew that the foundations of racial inequality will continue to exist until exploitation is ended. He saw that black and white workers are exploited by the same white capitalists and that victory for the exploited would depend upon black and white unity in struggle.

At the same time, Ben found that some reforms could be won under capitalism by mass struggle, even though these reforms are limited. He learned from the Herndon victory that it was possible to curb legal lynching by mass action. He also took part in the great struggles that abolished the white primary in the South and brought the ballot to many of the disfranchised in the former slave states. And he saw partial victories over the jim-crow system.

However, Ben understood well that these reforms were restricted. The terrible poverty of the black masses persisted. In fact, the misery of the people in the ghettos became worse with the mounting migration from the land to the cities, North and South. Furthermore, even the reforms won by struggle could be

misused and made to serve the system of exploitation unless constant vigilance and ever new struggles were maintained by the
masses. Nevertheless, Ben saw no need for a contradiction between the struggle for reform and the struggle for revolutionary
change in the basic structure of our society. He looked upon every
democratic victory won by the masses as a means of gaining
greater mass power for still greater struggles against the ex-
ploiters. This growing power could bring ultimate victory nearer.
But to accomplish this it would be necessary to imbue the masses
with the perspective of revolutionary change. That is why he
was a staunch and devoted Communist, who always believed in
the indispensable role of his party as a revolutionary force.

The elder Davis was able to give his son the kind of advanced
education available to few black youths. Ben attended Morehouse
in Atlanta, a Negro high school and college, and then took his
bachelor's degree at Amherst College, where he played on the
varsity football team. A law degree from Harvard came next. And
worldly success lay ahead for the young lawyer from Atlanta—if
he would pay the price.

The price was conformity. He must pattern himself after the
white rulers' image of a "good Negro" if he was to expect white
support. But that Ben would not do. His dignity and integrity
and his affection for his people stood in the way. And he knew
that the old ways would not help his people any more.

At this crucial point in his life, the South in which Ben was
living was very different from the plantation South of the last
century when his father's outlook was shaped. Big textile, chemi-
cal and metal fabricating plants were springing up in Atlanta
and other cities in Georgia. A huge iron and steel industry was
employing thousands of workers not far away in Birmingham,
including many former Negro sharecroppers. A black working
class was arising in the new South. Ben had but recently returned
from years of schooling in the North, where he felt the influences
of new values and felt the first stirrings that were to result in the
unionization of masses of black workers.

The way out was not yet clear in his mind, but Ben was re-
belling against the second-class citizenship from which all black

people suffered. He was outraged by lynchings of blacks and by the frame-up trials in the Atlanta courts that sent black people to the chain gangs. When the Republican Party, assuming that the son would follow in the father's footsteps, had offered him a lucrative post in the first election campaign of Herbert Hoover, he declined.

The case of Angelo Herndon was the turning point in Ben's life. The young Herndon had committed the worst crime in the jim-crow code. He brought black and white workers together to make demands on the white establishment. He was to be legally lynched under an old anti-insurrection law of Georgia, which carried the death penalty. The young attorney, then a novice barely embarked on the law business, volunteered to become Herndon's chief counsel. Deeply impressed by the courage and devotion of his client and his comrades, Ben joined the Communist Party during the defense campaign.

The Herndon campaign stirred millions, from all classes. But black and white workers, led by the Communist Party, became the core of the defense. That demonstration of the power of black and white unity was a decisive influence in Ben's life.

In the Communist Party, Ben developed as a Marxist thinker. He saw the capitalist monopolists as the chief enemies of the black people—and of the entire working class. They had to be defeated if black liberation was to be won and this could be done only by united struggle of the victims of monopoly, white and black.

True, Ben was never taken in by the Rockefellers' pretensions as "friends" of the Negro people. At first hand, he learned how they financed Atlanta University and other colleges and controlled Negro education. At the same time, they exploited black and white workers in industry and fleeced them through their banks and insurance companies. And all the while they kept on good terms with racist politicians. In later years, as a Communist leader in New York, when the Rockefeller family entered directly into politics, Ben was the first to expose their demogogy.

Ben always emphasized the need to unionize Southern industry as a blow against the Rockefellers and other monopolists, as well as against the base of the reactionary Dixiecrat bloc in Congress. This could not be done if the black workers were neglected or given second-class citizenship within the trade unions. He therefore urged unity of black and white workers as indispensible for a successful organizing drive in the South. That this was both practical and possible was shown in the timbermen's struggles in Louisiana, in the coal and iron mines and steel mills of Alabama, and on the docks of Southern port cities. After the Herndon victory when Ben came to New York, as an editor of the *Daily Worker* he wrote constantly about problems such as these, seeking ever higher levels of working class unity, as against separatist nationalist trends which came sharply forward during the Depression decade.

It was this approach that made possible Ben's successful election campaign for the New York City Council. His main base was what today would be called "black power"—in Harlem, where the masses rallied around him. But this black power base had white working class support. The campaign would not have been successful without the black base. Nor would it have achieved victory over the corrupt Tammany gang without the combined ballots of the black-white coalition.

Ben's team-mate in the City Council was Pete Cacchione, the beloved Italian-American Communist from Brooklyn who had been elected previously. Together, they won some good victories in the Council, among them rent control. The two Communists led the fight that forced the Tammany majority to pass the law which saved millions of dollars for New York tenants. And they kept racism on the defensive, taking up the battle against the Metropolitan Life Insurance Company and other lily-white landlords. They made racist cops watch their step. They took up the grievances of numerous citizens who came to them for relief. And they compelled the Council to pass a Davis resolution, giving official endorsement to Negro History Week.

Ben Davis died on August 22, 1964, after a long illness. Since his release from prison, he had been fully active as part of the national Communist leadership. He left a lovely and talented daughter, Emily. He also left us the memory of a selfless, dedicated comrade who was a model of courage not only in action but also in the quality of his critical and creative thinking.

The fight for black liberation, workers' rights and socialism now proceeds under new circumstances. There is a new upsurge in the country. New approaches and methods are forged in the struggle. Ben's natural milieu was struggle and one cannot help but think what great contributions he would have made today, together with his comrades, in helping provide leadership and a sense of direction to the great mass struggles of the present.

HENRY WINSTON

New York
October 1968

EDITOR'S NOTE

Benjamin J. Davis wrote his notes from day to day under the difficult conditions of prison life. He did not write a consecutive story, but rather essays, sketches and episodes which he intended to complete later. The notes were taken from him by the prison authorities as they were written. Thus he had no opportunity to edit his writings, much less construct a full autobiography, either while in prison nor after his release, since the manuscript was kept by the Bureau of Prisons until after his death.

When transcribed from his handwritten notes, the typed manuscript came to over 450 pages. It turned out that certain parts were written as more or less complete units—such as the chapters dealing with his early years, the Herndon case, the deaths of his father and of Pete Cacchione. He had also written at great length about his election to the City Council of New York and his work as a councilman. These sections appear much as they were written. Many repetitious passages—inevitable under the conditions of writing—as well as details of little interest to the general reader have been deleted. Separate pieces and themes which could not be fitted naturally into the consecutive story appear in the Appendix, and shorter extracts as footnotes in the text.

Unfortunately, there are important gaps. Undoubtedly the author had in mind that on his release from prison he would be able to fill in the story and otherwise complete his autobiography. Thus, nothing was found in his notes about his days at Amherst College, where he received his BA in 1925, or at Harvard Law School which awarded him his degree in 1932, outside some passing references. Under the constant eye of the prison warden, he no doubt felt it inopportune to write about his comrades and friends. In the manuscript turned over to his widow by the authorities, little was found about his suit to compel desegregation in prison. The entire period from 1936, when he gave up the practice of law to devote his full time to the Communist movement, and 1943, when he first ran for the city council, is left uncovered in his notes. It was during this period that he served as an editor of the *Daily Worker* and participated in the political work of the national Communist leadership as well as of the party in New York City, particularly in Harlem. Nor was anything found in the manuscript as received from the authorities about the Smith Act trial (outside some passing remarks).

Rather than attempt to fill in the gaps by inserting excerpts from his published writings of the time or by interviews with his contemporaries, it was thought best to present in as finished a form as possible the actual parts which were completed by the author. Since the author had no opportunity to edit his work, more than the usual editorial liberties have been taken, while exerting special care not to alter the substance of the manuscript.

COMMUNIST COUNCILMAN

FROM HARLEM

AUTHOR'S PREFACE

These autobiographical notes are written in the U.S. Federal Penitentiary at Terre Haute, Indiana. If the Truman administration had not jailed me and my fellow-Communist leaders, we would have been continuing our work for peace, freedom and socialism. The only possible compensation for this ordeal is that one has more time in prison to think about past experiences, to study, to reflect and—if the authorities permit—to write a book which may one day appear in print. In any case, the dreary and frustrating confinement sent me on a search for some definite undertaking to help break an oppressive monotony—which was all the more painful for being utterly senseless and undeserved.

Thus, it may have been my prison sentence that provided the occasion for this work, but its true origin and content come from deeper sources—out of life itself, out of my experiences and those of the Negro people as well as the white workers and progressives with whom I shared my Communist activities. There were many stories I had wanted to tell, many views I had long wanted to record, many questions at meetings to which there had seldom been opportunity to give adequate answers.

I write under the abnormal conditions of prison life, and my work may bear some of the earmarks of this stifling existence. In prison, anxieties over trifles become magnified into world-shaking problems, and one has to battle hard at times to maintain emotional equilibrium. The extremely limited contact with the outside world can cause one to become lopsided in his opinions. The reference material available in the prison library is scanty— especially on new developments in the United States and in the world. And, most of all, the absence of collective thinking, of the constant exchange of opinion with my comrades is the biggest single void in prison life. All of these handicaps may be reflected in a kind of self-centeredness, but I hope that in dealing with some of the highlights of my personal background, I may illuminate the lives of other Negro Americans and help in the struggle against imperialism, segregation and exploitation.

It is natural that I should dwell largely on topics dealing with Negro liberation. For this is the area of political activity in which, by choice, I have been most active. In a more fundamental sense, however, it is Marxism-Leninism which dominates my outlook on life, on history and the future. I have arrived at these views through 18 years of active membership in the Communist Party. Whatever modest contributions I have made to the struggles of the working class and of the Negro people must be attributed to my political convictions. And it helps to know that my party, despite the imprisonment of its leadership, is holding high its beacon light.

Even in jail, isolated from the rest of the population, one can feel the tension between the people's forces for peace and the minority monopolists for war. It is inevitable that this theme should thread its way through these pages, as it does through all my thinking. The struggle for peace is decisive for Negro and colonial freedom; it will be with us as long as capitalism, imperialism and human enslavement exist. The prison-enforced inability to participate actively in this supreme issue of our century throbs so acutely in one's mind that one is driven to find a task that has a meaning in this context.

Writing these pages, then, gives me an opportunity to look back at my origins, my childhood in Georgia, the remarkable man who was my father—as well as to put down many of the ideas I need to examine objectively. The notes are necessarily incomplete, but I hope that those who are interested in truth and progress may find enough substance in them to spur their search for the free America of tomorrow.

CHAPTER ONE

THE WORLD I WAS BORN INTO

At the turn of the century, Dawson, Georgia, was a quaint typical Southern town of about five to ten thousand in southwest Georgia. It was surrounded by big plantations that drew their workers largely from the Negro population.

The town itself was checkered with cotton patches, corn fields and pigpens as numerous as the wooden frame shacks. During the day, in cotton-picking time, one could ride through Dawson and see scores of Negroes in the cotton patches with huge sacks on their backs, picking cotton from sunup to sundown—men, women and children, young and old.

The Negro population was a third to a half of the white. They picked cotton, tilled the soil, tended the pigpens, drove the horses and took care of all the menial work. The women were domestic servants, mainly cooks, housekeepers and nurses—including wet nurses.

The small business district consisted of eight to ten rural blocks in the white section of the town, with some large country stores including a hardware store, the town hall and a few other buildings. Negroes were always puttering around at janitorial tasks, for which they were paid partly in money, partly in cast-off clothing and other goods—and partly in a false sense of security. The whole town had the atmosphere of a feudal plantation.

One of the things I remember most vividly was the way the town was set up. The tracks of the railroad—the Seaboard Airline—were the dividing line. The Negroes lived on one side, the whites on the other, except for a small colony of Negro families who lived near the business area. There weren't more than five or six of these, and their "excuse" for living there was their connection with the few places of business which Negroes were

compelled to patronize—the barber shop, the undertaking establishment, and the like.

The white section of Dawson was clean; the sidewalks planted
with cool trees; the dirt streets were smooth and well-groomed.
There were no pavements. The Negro section was like an extension of the dirty railroad yard of the Seaboard. No trees separated
the sidewalk from the street; the whole area was a slum.

Dawson was peaceful. It was the peace of the master's domination over the slave; the kind of peace that white supremacists say
is disturbed when Negroes become restless for their rights. No-
body talked about the Constitution of the United States or, for
that matter, that of Georgia—least of all the Negroes. No Negro
mentioned voting, or running for office, or higher wages, or
equality before the law, or decent schools, or manhood status.
That would disturb the peace, and everyone was getting on fine
—white with Negro, and Negro with white. The Negroes knew
very well that the U.S. Constitution had no bearing in Georgia.
They knew that the law was what the "white folks" said it was.
It was true that the slaves had been freed, and that the 13th,
14th and 15th Amendments had been added to the Constitution,
but no one thought seriously of letting this interfere with Dawson's peaceful quaintness.

Here is where I was born. So were all my relatives before me,
as far as records and the memory of Negro men and women
could go.

We lived in a big two-story house in the center of the Negro
residential district, about a mile from the railroad tracks in one
direction, and about a mile from the main Negro church—Sardis
Baptist—in the other. There was a white picket fence around
our house, separating it from a large cotton patch on both sides.
It was on the corner. There was a large playing yard, a big pig-
pen filled with pigs, and a rather ornate outhouse about 25 yards
from the house. When I became conscious of my identity, my
father was already on his way toward a successful career in the
Negro fraternal field. He had bought the house from a white
family—one of the last to leave the Negro side of the railroad
tracks. Down the road a piece, right across from Sardis Baptist

Church, lived a rather well-off Negro family—the head of the household an insurance agent. But all around were the poorest of families, who lived in railroad shacks of three rooms, broken down and impossible to tell one from another. I often wondered how their owners did.

About a 100 yards from us lived my uncle John, his wife Dinkie, my aunt Mollie—the only living sister of my dad—and my grandmother, a truly venerable and remarkable woman. All these were on my father's side. My playmates were Lee and Tom Mulky, sons of my aunt Mollie, and kids from all around the neighborhood.

My uncle John was a carpenter by trade; he'd never seen a school. He lived until he was 100 or close to it (he died in 1952). In Bronwood, Georgia, lived my uncle Mike and his large family. He was a sharecropper and remained inseparable from the land until his death in 1953. (Bronwood was seven miles from Dawson, near Americus, where Rosa Ingram and her two sons were sentenced to death in 1949; she had refused to become the concubine of a rich white planter, who was killed when he attempted to impose his attentions upon her.)

Uncle Mike Davis was tall, black and handsome, about six feet three inches in height, slender, with a slight stoop in his shoulders from long, backbreaking hours on the master's plantation. Often he would send a mule and wagon for me in Dawson. I would go to Bronwood, pick cotton and become part of his large working household.

My paternal grandmother was Katherine Davis. She had a beautiful dark face and was of ordinary stature, but the pride and dignity of her personality made her seem a much larger woman. She was the head of our clan, so to speak, and none dared to cross her, not even her oldest sons, including my dad. She maintained an unbelievable impartial justice toward the whole family. My sister was named for her.

Grandma Davis was born in slavery, as were her oldest sons John and Mike. She bore its marks to her grave. She died in 1924, while I was at college. During her young womanhood she was beaten within an inch of her life by a sadistic slave master.

She had suffered many brutal whippings as a slave, because of
the fierce and militant protectiveness she exercised over her
family. "I wasn't going to let 'em kill my children," she would
say, as she told her grandchildren the story. As a result of the
beatings she was permanently crippled. Her right leg was stiff
at the knee joint and couldn't be bent. As my father grew financially able, he sent her to many specialists, but they said it was
hopeless.

We never knew our paternal grandfather; I don't think any
of grandma's children knew him. I used to ply grandma with
questions, but she never liked to talk about him. When she did,
tears would come to her wrinkled eyes; it was a story that brought
back the brutality and barbarism of the slave system. My grandfather, she said, was a very militant fellow who could never quite
reconcile himself to slavery. He was defiant, constantly in trouble, a bad example for the other slaves, and impudent to his
owner. He always wanted to be "somebody." And when I would
ask her what she meant by that, she would say sweetly: "I don't
know. I guess he wanted to be a man." Then she would add:
"Your father is more like him than any of my children." She
meant that father was her favorite son.

"One day," she said, "he was defending me from a whipping.
So the master started to whip him instead of me. He must have
beaten him half a day, trying to force him to say that he would
never interfere with any more whippings I got. But they couldn't
break him. . . . They almost killed him though. A few days later
the master sold him away from us, and neither I nor the children
ever saw him again."

Grandma could not read or write, neither could Uncle John
or Uncle Mike. I used to read to them when I was about nine or
ten. It was her pride and joy that her grandchildren could read
and write, were being educated. Grandma really belonged to the
matriarchal period in the development of the Negro family. Frequently fathers were sold away from their families, especially if
they were young and healthy. But mothers were kept with their
young children, as an investment, to insure their "bringing up."
These mothers became the "fathers," too, and ruled over their

families with authority and responsibility, and, like grandma, with iron discipline. I could see that in the respect that my uncles, my father and aunt Molly had for her. She was a woman of character and determination.

On my mother's side, I knew my grandmother and two of my mother's sisters. I have a faint recollection of my grandfather, who was quite dark and of medium build. My mother had no full sisters or brothers—she was the only child of my grandmother's second marriage. My maternal grandmother was extremely fair, with coarse gray hair that hung below her waist when she let it down. My maternal aunts Addie and Rossie were also fair, with coarse black hair. Mother was light brown, with soft rounded features, big eyes, and a splendid, straight carriage.

Often mother took me to see grandmother, who was a domestic for a rich white family on the other side of the railroad tracks. Grandmother "slept in," as she had been doing with the same family for a quarter of a century. Mother, too, was a domestic when she and my father met. Grandmother died before I was old enough to form a friendship with her. My mother's family line remained shadowy to me.

The railroad tracks separated two entirely different worlds— the white and the black. I remember little about the former. Mother never went across the tracks except, on rare occasions, to purchase what was not available on the black side, or to visit grandmother. I recall vividly going across on one occasion to see the circus. The white children's county school was in the town proper. But the Negro children's school was at a considerable distance in the country, as if it offended the delicate sensibilities of the whites to countenance the children of their slaves going to school.

When I was about four, I attended the Negro school for one "term." Actually, the session lasted about six weeks early in the spring. There were only ten or 15 of us in the ramshackle, wooden-frame house with one room—a hazard to life and limb and utterly unusable in bad weather, even if it had been possible to reach it through the mud and slush of backwoods roads and fields. Mother and father finally decided against my going there

—which became one of the principal reasons why the family migrated "north" to Atlanta.

Dawson still reeked with the stench of the slave market. It was only 40-odd years since the Emancipation Proclamation. The master-slave relation between Negro and white was vivid in the minds of more than half of the Negro population, many of whom had been slaves. They were looked upon and treated by the whites as if they were chattels still belonging to their white masters. One of the origins of present-day segregation could be clearly seen in the kind of railroad-track division in all the Dawsons of the deep South. In slavery times, the masters lived in the "big house," which was clearly separated from the slave shacks, far removed out on the plantation. The Negro side of the Seaboard tracks in 1903 was like the slave hovels of 1860.

The peace of the town was broken only when the sheriff and a load of deputies came across the tracks to pick up some helpless Negro. On one such occasion, I remember, a Negro man had "sassed" a white in the downtown area. The next day the "wagon" came to pick him up. Everyone on the Negro side of the tracks knew about it—the news traveled as it had on the slave plantation. The road all the way to the victim's house was lined with men, women and children. The wagon passed right in front of my house, and I stood in front of the picket fence watching the proceedings. It looked like a parade, on the one hand, and a funeral, on the other. Men, women and children were sobbing. Mother explained what had happened and what was involved. "They say," she told me, "he didn't behave himself downtown." The people sobbed because Negroes usually got long terms on the county chain gang, whose brutality was beyond imagination. Many didn't survive. Those who resisted such inhuman mistreatment were labeled "crazy," as were all Negroes foolish enough to talk or act like a man or woman.

The health and medical services for Negroes in Dawson were practically nil. There was one Negro doctor in the town and no dentist. On rare occasions, a Negro family might get the services of a benevolent and patronizing white physician. But it had to be a very special family for that rare privilege. Like most Negro mothers, mine, too, was victimized by this lack of facilities. Had all my brothers and sisters lived, we would have had a large family. The first child, Benny Will, died at three, victim of a hemorrhage which could easily have been stopped with minimal medical attention. Then there were twins—boys—one of whom was born dead; the other died a few weeks afterward as a result of neglect at birth. My sister and myself miraculously pulled through. Infant mortality was so common among Negro families that a healthy birth was the occasion for celebration. This was one of the conditions that drove my father out of Dawson.

As an individual, my father was militant, aggressive, ambitious and of strong determination. These qualities extended to his concern for his family. Educational and manhood opportunities for his family and for himself were nil in Dawson. He wanted to strike out for greener pastures, and his chance came through his connection with the Grand United Order of Odd Fellows, in which he made rapid strides to the top. From this point he branched into politics through the Republican Party. This led him to Atlanta, 200 miles farther north—his political and fraternal headquarters. He would return to Dawson two or three times a month to be with the family. Then, about 1909, we moved north to Atlanta, shaking the dust of ante-bellum Dawson from our feet forever.

The way of progress for the Negro in those days was in alliance with the "better class" of whites, that is, with liberal capitalists, do-good philanthropists, and occasional Southern bourbons who maintained an attitude of benevolence toward their former slaves. But this extended only to individual Negroes—not to Negroes as an oppressed people. Indeed, it often was at the expense of the latter. In Dawson, for example, Negroes got along within the framework of the jim-crow system with a certain immunity, if they were fortunate enough to have a rich white benefactor or sponsor who would take care of them in emergencies as he would his favorite cow or horse or mule. Such a Negro was a good workman, who knew his place. Such a Negro had all sorts of license in his actions against other Negroes, whom he could even kill, and "Mr. Charlie" would get him out of it. But the same Negro did not even have a minimum of citizenship rights in relation to a white person. And it wasn't often that his big white boss would stand up for his protégé if he was "sassy" or "crazy" enough to challenge white supremacy.

This is very much like the Negro police system that I saw in Daytona Beach, Florida, when I was visiting a boyhood chum, Albert Bethune, some years ago. There, two or three Negroes were members of the local police force. They could arrest any Negro, but they dared not lay a hand upon a white citizen. On the other hand, any white civilian could arrest a Negro policeman. The Negro policemen were in truth "Keystone cops."

My father was on good terms with the "right white people" in Dawson. But his career was advancing so rapidly that it would soon have brought him into a clash with them. Moving to Atlanta gave him a little more elbow room. Father was a product of the Negro-big-capital era and was, in a sense, its prisoner. Marx somewhere said that no leader can go beyond the period in which he lived. Father fought doggedly on elementary questions of the right of the Negro people to vote, hold office and enjoy the rights of citizenship—but he always fought within the existing framework. This is the line he followed throughout his life. He did not change in this, even though his life span included about 15 years of the Negro-labor period of collaboration.

The early years of my life in Atlanta followed a middle-class standard of living which was the consequence of my father's economic success. Naturally, this, in some degree, spared me some of the social burdens and handicaps of the jim-crow system. I attended Summer Hill public school from the first to the sixth grades. It was, of course, segregated. There were no sidewalks, and I can remember wading through seas of mud whenever it rained. The teachers and the principal were all Negro.

In fact, from my birth in Dawson until I finished public school in Atlanta, I lived in a world entirely apart from white Americans—I lived in the Negro-American world. I went to Negro churches, played with Negro children, went to segregated Negro schools, lived in a ghetto with Negro drug stores, barber shops, movies, haberdasheries, and so on. White people were a strange lot to me. The only contact I had with them was hateful. I regarded them as colorless—especially physically—somewhat inferior, wicked and authoritarian. I observed them as policemen —bosses with no other mission in life but to oppress, arrest and mistreat Negroes. Such was my experience—the only experience afforded by the social setup of the "free world" of the early 1900's. Such was the experience of every Negro kid, and it drew us together in a strong common bond—one that binds all Negroes together, irrespective of social position, age, sex, color, creed, political affiliation or economic status.

Any fool could figure out that the Negroes were not responsible for this attitude, nor for the conditions that gave rise to it. The difference in our psychology and attitudes as Negroes—the thing that sets all Negroes apart from other Americans—is plainly the oppression of the Negroes as a people. And I was reared in the Black Belt or on its immediate periphery, living in the heartland of the territory where national oppression was most severe, where the lynch rope and intimidation were the "rule of law" that governed black men and women.

And my contemporary, the white child, was being taught that the Negro was inferior, that the Negro's "natural place" was as the servitor of the white man, that he was a beast of burden. Chief Justice Taney's dictum that the Negro had no rights that the white man was bound to respect was the white man's code of honor transmitted to his children with their mother's milk. The difference in the white child's feeling of superiority and my own (for I did have such a feeling) was that his was based upon the subservient position of the Negro as it existed in life itself, while mine was wholly removed from the reality that the Negro held a second-class position in this world. He was no more in a position to reverse this situation than a lamb was to assert dominance over a lion.

But living in this Negro world, I learned its beauties and its strengths, too—its inherent ability and power to fight for its own eventual liberation. I learned its own ordered system of existence. It had its leaders, its masses of hard-working people, its culture, its rich and its poor, its scholars, artists, music and literature, its militant traditions, its ambitions, its builders, its educational institutions, its statesmen and scientists, its own codes of life. I learned to appreciate these attributes and to be proud of them.

CHAPTER TWO

A SOUTHERN EDUCATION

Atlanta was the cultural center of the Southern Negro, sharing that distinction with Nashville, Tennessee. Respectable institutions of higher education were situated in Atlanta, the best known among them being Atlanta University and Morehouse College. Spelman College was an all-girls seminary associated with Morehouse, although no more than a dozen or so Spelman students would go to Morehouse for a college degree. Spelman derived its name from Laura Spelman Rockefeller, whose family endowed the institution in her name. When, in the twenties, Florence Read—a white woman—became president of Spelman, she came to the position directly out of the Rockefeller establishment. Later, after 1929 when the Atlanta University system was established to include all the Negro institutions of higher learning, she became a kingpin of Negro education in Atlanta.*

There were no public high schools for Negro youth in my

* The Rockefeller octopus gobbled up the Negro eductional system, as it gobbled up business competitors during the economic depression. Miss Read did her job well. Atlanta University became the graduate institution for all the Negro colleges in Atlanta. John Hope, who had been Morehouse president, became president of the new system, while Miss Read, as treasurer, was virtually dictator. Big business took charge, with its new buildings, redecorated campuses, kept faculties and controlled students' minds. The white supremacy structure in the South welcomed this development, since it helped perpetuate the fiction of "separate but equal" education, a cornerstone of segregation. It was also welcomed by Northern universities, which were relieved of the growing pressure from Negro applicants. But it wasn't long before pressure was renewed upon the conservative and hesitant NAACP to undertake legal actions for the entrance of Negroes into state-supported colleges in the South. The Negro College Fund was then organized to retain the hold of big business over Negro institutions in the South.

31

time. All the Negro colleges were therefore compelled to maintain high school, normal or academy departments. Some carried a couple of years of grade school, to ease the transition from public to high school. Atlanta University maintained Oglethorpe as a private grade school, and Morehouse maintained two years of grade school—to seventh and eighth grades. These were the two leading Negro institutions. When I left Summer Hill public school at the conclusion of the sixth grade, I entered Morehouse for the seventh and eighth, and I remained there for four years of high school and one year of college.

It seemed as natural to my father that I should attend Morehouse, rather than Atlanta, as it was that I was his son. I preferred Morehouse—its football fame was far and beyond the others. But my preference at this age was hardly decisive, to put it mildly.

There were certain secondary considerations which entered my father's thinking. He was a self-made man, and he thought his own upbringing was the only path to individual success and achievement. While he was determined that my sister and I should get the best education possible, he was, by the same token, afraid of any softness of character that our relatively high standard of living might engender. He was constantly haunted by the specter of an indulged, good-for-nothing son. I heard this note in every disagreement between us, every time he disapproved of me. He wanted to balance my easy life at home with hard, tough discipline. He figured that Morehouse with its rough-and-ready boys' student body was better suited to his aim than Atlanta University, a co-educational institution. What was more, he wanted to get me away from having a car at my disposal, and the like.

So I entered Morehouse as a boarding student, living on the campus, with all the restrictions the other boys had (one had to get a permit to leave the campus), eating the same plain, modest fare—with no more privileges than the poorest farmer's son from the backwoods of Georgia. The students at Morehouse were, by and large, sons of poor parents, with quite a few working their way through. I was a boarding student for the entire seven years

I attended, going across town to my home once or twice a month to spend weekends. This was the only departure from the rigors of boarding-in that my father would countenance. Other privileges—such as traveling with the football team—had to be vigorously fought for.

Thus, while students at Morehouse were often sons of field hands, Atlanta University was the school of the Negro aristocracy, numbering among its students the sons and daughters of Atlanta's and Georgia's Negro upper class. All of these exclusive families did not derive their aristocratic status from wealth. There were other characteristics which this élite had in common. In some cases they were the direct descendants of white slaveowners who had provided well for the illegitimate Negro wings of their families. The fathers and mothers of AU students often had enjoyed the advantages of education—at a time when education alone was sufficient to mark the Negro as an aristocrat. One other attribute they all had in common—they were light-complexioned, some absolutely undistinguishable from whites. They associated with no dark brethren socially and intermarried among their own color. There was a period in the Negro's development when color alone was the criterion of social position. My school days in Atlanta coincided with the twilight of the Negro's color-based aristocracy. The inexorable necessities of economic law finally knocked it into a cocked hat. A dark Negro would break into the exclusive color circle, leaving his new in-laws a little chagrined but a little wealthier.

The other thing these people had in common was religious denomination. Most of them were Congregationalists or Episcopalians. My family were Baptists, along with the Methodists the denomination of the masses. Morehouse was Baptist-sponsored; Atlanta was Congregationalist-sponsored.

A bitter foe of every type of social exclusiveness, father expressed this in sending me to Morehouse. His most vitriolic public adversaries were to be found among the light-complexioned aristocrats. Father fought in the Republican Party for rank-and-file control on questions of voting and civil rights for the masses. He fought for an independent Negro business community, as he did for Negro doctors and lawyers, and for increased purchasing power for the Negro workers and farmers.

The colored élite displayed no concern for the Negro masses, to whom father sought to give a sense of their great strength. He made the Negro community his first concern, trying to elevate its dignity and building its consciousness—entirely within a middle-class framework, to be sure—the limit of his vision in his heyday. Thus, he represented the ascending Negro middle class, while the social élite of color and inherited material possessions was in decline. Rising to replace this élite was a Negro middle class of lawyers, doctors, business and professional men.

The Negro masses, whom the aristocrats excluded—even while collecting rents from them—were my father's daily associates. It was their world of which he was a part. The aristocrats lived on an island, but it was nourished by the work of the masses.

The new period, which father heralded, needed capital and investment for the Negro economy. The social élite did not have this capital; it could only be accumulated by organization of the Negro masses into fraternal societies and businesses, with the farmer playing a dominant role. Accumulation had to come from the workers and sharecroppers, tenant farmers and the like. The first dramatic sign of Negro business enterprise in Atlanta was the Odd Fellows block, built by the Grand United Order of Odd Fellows with the nickels and dimes of its tens of thousands of members. Morehouse was the symbol of this rising, democratic-minded middle class—in its outlook, its composition and its atmosphere. Since the 1920's, its graduates were playing a role in the professions, and particularly in business.

The seven years at Morehouse were spent during a highly formative period of my youth. The sun rose and set in Morehouse, and it was here that my democratic orientation toward life received its grounding. Here, too, I learned more about my people, their potentialities and talents. The seven years served to seal off my mind further from whites—except as unknown and repressive strangers. Along with my studies, I learned human warmth. I also learned that Negroes ran colleges as efficiently as anyone and that Negro students—far from being "shiftless," as the slanderous white supremacists maintained—were full of ambition and high purpose.

I learned, too, what a "religious atmosphere" is—the meaningful phrase that still adorns the ads of Southern Negro institutions in *The Crisis*. In practice, a religious atmosphere is one in which free thought is forbidden. If religion is designed to deaden the militant dissatisfaction of the masses, it also becomes a potent weapon in wangling donations from white philanthropists who are titillated at the sight of a "healthy corps of religious, spiritual-singing Negroes." Negro college presidents became past masters in the use of this weapon. (Such are the blessings of Christianity.)

This singing of spirituals for money was to me undignified, subservient and a perversion of indigenous Negro folk music. It helped to awaken my indignation at the exploitation of Negroes by whites and, in this case, at the misuse of the talents of Negroes. I wondered why these philanthropists were not equally eager to find students who were brilliant mathematicians and to offer them jobs as actuarial accountants in, say, the Metropolitan Life Insurance Company. Didn't these fellows count unless they could sing "Swing Low, Sweet Chariot?" It was a subtle way of telling the young Negro that no matter what he learned and how well he learned it, he was still a singer of religious spirituals at the bidding of the master.

But John Hope, then the president of Morehouse, knew which side his bread was buttered on. The students would joke about it. When we had performed in chapel, one of us would ask the other: "I wonder if we'll get that new building now." The practice all but turned me against Negro spirituals forever. It wasn't until years later, when I heard them in their true context—in the working class and Negro people's movements—that I realize their profound and positive value.

Those students—and they were rare indeed—who broke from the pattern of conformity paid the price. First, they were raked over the coals by the faculty; then the student body devised its own unofficial punishment. I remember one such instance of an extraordinarily brilliant young fellow, believed to be a mathematical genius, who confounded faculty and students alike with

his mental wizardry in many other subjects as well. He was a
normal lad in every way, but he did not bother to be diplomatic,
expressing himself with a kind of raw, naive bluntness. His cardinal sin was that he was an atheist and made no bones about it.
He would engage the professors on this point—much to their
discomfort and embarrassment. They used to classify him as
"crazy," but his scholarship made this an ineffectual means of
discrediting him.

A group of student leaders decided to hold a meeting to discuss his case. It was to take the form of a funeral, in which one
of the leaders was to "preach his soul to heaven." The event
finally took place, the victim willingly participating as the
"corpse." There were sermons—the tenor of which was that the
young man had passed into another world and was no longer a
part of ours.

The whole thing was done in the spirit of fun one day right
after dinner. It was attended by the entire student body—except
me. I watched the proceedings from my dormitory window for a
while, then became disgusted. It purported to be fun, but it
wasn't. It was the method chosen by the student leadership to
demonstrate to the faculty that it disassociated itself from the
radical, atheistic views of the rebel.

I later became very friendly with him, and we spent many
hours in unorthodox discussions. Many months later, he left
Morehouse; he didn't fit in with its "religious atmosphere."
(About 11 years later we met again. He had studied law and
hadn't lost any of his radical views on life. I wanted him to come
into my office, and he did for a while. Always in frail health,
however, he died before our partnership was consummated.)

Students in the Negro colleges of the South at that time were
of much higher age levels than now—or, for that matter, than in
white colleges. Negro families found it much more difficult to
send their children to school, and educational facilities for the
farmers' children were a hundred times more difficult. Negro
students often had to wait to enter college until they were of an
age where they could either materially aid their fathers and
mothers or wholly finance themselves. Consequently, over half

the students at Morehouse were 23 or over. Some juniors and
seniors were 30 or over. My associations were largely with these
older men. So that at an early age, my ideas and approach to life
became prematurely serious and solemn.

I soon developed a rebellious attitude toward unreasonable
discipline. During World War I, the faculty instituted a rule
that students would no longer be permitted to study in their
dormitory rooms but that immediately after supper all students
were to come to study hall for two hours. It was a wholly unreasonable regulation that just about wiped out student freedom.
Study hall was to be conducted by faculty members—thus giving
the faculty supervision over the students from the time they got
up in the morning until 10 at night.

A group of us got together to fight this rule. I was 14 or 15,
while other members of the group were in their twenties. We
sent a petition to the faculty, which accomplished nothing. The
faculty re-affirmed the regulation and threatened anyone who
disobeyed it or agitated against it.

Our group quickly formed itself into a committee—later
branded by the faculty as a "conspiracy against the Christian
principles and authority of the institution." It was ordered dis-
banded.

But we reacted instantly with several student mass meetings
in each dormitory, where we explained the issues and set up an
illegal committee. We won the support of the students, all of
whom regarded the study hall as oppressive, especially since most
of them were grown men. Then we called a student strike and
refused to attend any classes until the study hall was abolished.

The faculty was thrown into a panic. The strike was solid,
lasting three or four days, with neither side budging. The faculty
called a student meeting in chapel, requiring full attendance, to
discuss the situation. We went, in the expectation of a favorable
settlement—since the school had been shut down. Instead, we
got a harangue from John Davis about the "spirit of Morehouse."
But Davis was a most popular faculty member and had an influence over a large section of the student body; the pressure to end
the strike was too powerful for us to hold out. In a couple of days

students trickled back to classes. We organized squads to talk to "weak links," but the "back-to-class" movement had snowed us under. The faculty had turned on the red-baiting and intimidation; termed us "godless," "Bolsheviks," likening us to the Reds in Russia, who were featured daily in the front news (they had just completed the October Revolution).

The faculty met and expelled all the ringleaders—our entire committee, in the first place. I was one of the first. The dean called in each of us. When my turn came, he declared that I couldn't run the school, that I was getting into bad company, that soon I would be just like that mathematical genius who didn't believe in God. I replied I didn't see what that had to do with the fact that the methods of a kindergarten were being imposed upon grown men, some as old as faculty members. Too bad, he replied, I had to leave. So I went, happy to return home, happier still that I had stood up, at 14, for what I thought right.

At my unexpected arrival, Dad had about fifty fits. Mother was amused, but father cussed me out: "I didn't have the proper respect for authority," and to on. I "was going to end up in jail" (he was right about that). I replied then as I would today. I had no respect for authority except when it was just and right—in this instance, authority was wrong. This question of blind respect for authority remained a matter of cleavage between my father and me, the dividing line between our philosophies of life. (It once burst into the open when Calvin Coolidge, then governor of Massachusetts, banned a Boston police strike on the ground that "no one can strike against the government." My father, taking a highly partisan Republican view, upheld Coolidge, and I wrote an article in the *Independent,* supporting the police and condemning Coolidge.)

Father reserved his choicest invectives, however, for the Morehouse faculty administration. He blasted them for expelling his son, not hesitating to exploit his own prominent position. Whereupon the faculty changed my expulsion to suspension and I was back in Morehouse in about three weeks.

Meantime, the strike was lost—but the war was won. A few days after I returned, the faculty withdrew the study hall regulation, and no such unreasonable provision was again imposed on the student body while I was there. It was my first venture into public battle on a collective basis. And I enjoyed it more than any other experience in my entire stay at Morehouse. The fact that it had been a struggle waged against Negroes indicated quite clearly to me that issues are issues and that they sometimes cut across racial lines. While white oppression existed everywhere, certain Negroes in relation to others had to be opposed. A philosophy of life was germinating in my youthful mind.

CHAPTER THREE

I BECOME A LAWYER

After finishing my law course at Harvard, I did not enter immediately into the practice of my profession. I detoured into the field of journalism.

Actually I had never been too keen on the law. From my earliest school days, I was much more enamored of the arts—music in particular. I fancied I possessed considerable talent in this field—much more than I really had—but I did recognize that I was no genius. My father succeeded in persuading me to try to study law, but I did it without bursting enthusiasm. By the time I got out of law school, I was pretty weary of school in general and law in particular. I had been attending school every year from the time I was six until I was twenty-five. And these 19 years had brought me no closer, I thought, to the solution of the problem that hammered at me every day—the securing of my birthright as a free and equal American citizen. In many respects the problem had even been intensified in school. The contradiction set up within me was between the rare luck of my being able to attend such highly rated institutions and the inferior status imposed upon me by the society of which Amherst and Harvard were social pillars.

A vivid example of this comes to mind. My first year's schooling in the East was at Amherst College, an exclusive New England institution, where I made the varsity football team. But that very summer, during my vacation in Atlanta, I was arrested and man-handled by the police because I sat in the "white section" of the trolley car, after I had given my seat to a pregnant Negro woman. I had violated the jim-crow laws enforced to "keep niggers in their place." I shall never forget the incident. The rednecked cop grabbed me by the belt of my pants and yanked me off the trolley in the white business section of the city, as if I were a desperado. The Negro women on the trolley screamed. They were all called disorderly, ejected from the car, and shooed away as if they were chattels.

I was wearing a black sweater with a purple "A" on it—the regulation varsity letter awarded at Amherst. The cop asked me what the letter stood for, and I told him. It was as if I were speaking Greek—he'd never heard of it, and his ignorance made him even more vicious. He asked me who I was, and I told him. He recognized my father's name and then muttered under his breath about "sending niggers up north to school." He did not jail me, however, although the "Black Maria" came. He gave me a summons to be at court the next morning at 10 o'clock.

The next day my father went with me. It was a police court located on Decatur Street, around the corner from the County Court House. We sat in the Negro section in the rear, awaiting my turn. What I heard during the long wait was enough to shock the most insensitive. The police court provided a form of entertainment, of sport, for the petty officials, at the expense of the hapless, humble Negro workers caught in the complicated toils of jim-crow laws. The vulgarity of the tin-horn magistrate was repellent, while the police and their hangers-on stood around making merry. One Negro woman was virtually stripped bare by the lewd language and gestures of the magistrate. The clerks and bailiffs fingered the woman's breasts as she stood there helplessly, her face bathed in tears of shame and agony.

I remarked to my dad that I had never seen such obscene behavior. I was boiling. He said: "That's why I want you to be a lawyer. Maybe you can defend your people some day from this sort of thing." The law was the greatest of all professions to my father, and he always wanted me to be a lawyer. I often felt he was trying to achieve his own life's ambition through me.

When my case was finally called, father and I walked to the bench. The cop gave his version of the happening, and I started to give mine. The magistrate refused to listen. Instead, he turned to my father, who said: "My son has never been arrested before. He thought he was doing right and had no evil intent. He told me what happened and explained that he felt compassion for a pregnant woman who he thought was ill. He gave her his seat and then sat down in the wrong section of the car. He offered no resistance to the officer. I ask you to excuse him this time and parole him in my custody."

I started again to speak but father nudged me.

The wizened, ignorant, tobacco-chewing magistrate then delivered a lecture.

"Ben," addressing my father (Negroes were never addressed as Mr. or Mrs.), "you're starting your boy off on the wrong track. You sent him up no'th to school and he comes back thinking he's as good as a white man. You better get that stuff out of his head or we'll knock it out. You know the ropes here—this is a white man's country—no matter what it is up no'th. I'm gonna let him off this time, but I warn you we ain't gonna have no niggers down here sitting down with white people. Ten days or ten dollars. As a favor to you, Ben, pay the ten dollars and I'll suspend sentence."

My father gulped audibly—swallowing his pride. He reached into his pocket, paid the fine, and we walked out of the courtroom.

I was furious. At the same time I felt ashamed and humiliated —not so much for myself as for my father and my people. If this could happen to me—the son of a well-to-do Negro—what, indeed, would have been the fate of a Negro who had failed to get himself born into a "well-to-do" family?

Nothing I studied at Amherst or later at Harvard gave me the solution to this question; nor was full dignity and citizenship given me at either institution. I was taught the art of being "a free American gentleman," but in life I was treated as an inferior. It didn't make sense. And though I didn't see the way out at that time, I never resigned myself to inferior status. I remained dissatisfied, basically unhappy, and in my own way continued to suspend judgment on the purpose of my life until the time when I found some answer to this gnawing contradiction.

When I returned to Atlanta after my final year at law school, my father wanted me to enter the office of a Negro assistant federal attorney in Illinois. But I demurred: I wanted to look around a bit.

Finally, I consented to enter a firm of publishers' representatives that secured national advertisements for my father's paper, the *Atlanta Independent*. This firm was white and had a monopoly on national advertising in the Negro newspaper field. It received a commission on all the national advertising in the Negro papers. I had some familiarity with the newspaper field, through working on father's paper. But I was completely unfamiliar with the approach of a publisher's representative.

Soon after I entered this firm, I became editor of the "Illustrated Feature Section," a syndicated weekly insert which was carried by most of the Negro press, including the *Atlanta Independent*. It was printed centrally in Chicago. The insert carried advertisements, the profits from which were theoretically prorated among the Negro newspapers in proportion to their circulation. My job was to edit the literary material and to supervise the publication of the insert. I remained at this work from 1929 to the middle of 1931. My offices were in Chicago and then in Baltimore, in the headquarters of the Baltimore *Afro-American*. Subsequently, I returned to Atlanta.

The incident that caused me to give up this work is perhaps worth mentioning. My firm had sought through its weekly insert feature to secure a stranglehold on the entire Negro newspaper field—a fact which became clear to me as I went along. But some of the papers balked; they wouldn't go along. The firm then thought up another scheme. It proposed to establish a news service, to corner the Negro news market, much as the Associated Press and the United Press have done in the white newspaper field, and then refuse news to any paper that did not retain it as publisher's representative. It was a fabulous scheme, and if it had worked, it would have bottled up the entire Negro newspaper field, with the stopper in the company's hand.

They proposed that I should be the front for the scheme. They would supply the money, and I, my name and prestige as a Negro—which meant the name and prestige of my father.

I wanted no part of it, and I quit. I didn't relish seeing myself used to undermine the independence of the Negro press for a mess of pottage. It was an instinctive reaction on my part. I did not yet have a conscious political feeling about such matters—except that it seemed an insult to me as an individual and to my sense of racial dignity. My father owned a newspaper which I had learned to respect, and there were many others which possessed what my father called "character and soul." Any dishonor to these papers would not be by my hand. Moreover, I was resentful and felt insulted that I should have been requested to play such a role.

My resignation ended a brief phase of my life that followed the end of my formal education. The quest for an answer to my problems had taken me through college and law school into practical journalism; from Atlanta to Massachusetts, to Illinois and Maryland and back to Atlanta, but I had not found the "holy grail." I was, as it were, suspended in midair. I might as well, I reasoned, begin the practice of law. So I did, in January of 1932.

I began to practice law in Atlanta, after having been admitted to the Georgia bar. It wasn't so much that I wanted to practice law but that I was profoundly influenced by the conditions of 1932—the great depression and its devastating effects upon my own people. These entered into my thinking and concerned me more than the actual practice of the law—with its pleadings and technicalities. In short, I entered upon the practice of my profession with mixed motivations—idealistic and humanitarian aspirations, as well as the need for a career. After all, I had devoted years to the study of the law. All these elements overlapped; some of them were contradictory. But I had no illusions about becoming a Brandeis, Holmes or Cardozo—the only members of the Supreme Court for whom I had much respect while at law school. The realities of my color dashed any such aspirations. But I was challenged by the thought of what could be done if one put up a really tough fight for the constitutional rights of Negroes in a Georgia court and was himself a Negro lawyer.

I had brushed up on the law in the office of Attorneys Walden and Henry before I took the Georgia bar examination. I shall never forget the kindness of both during that period, nor of their secretary, Rachel Pruden, herself now a member of the bar, the first Negro woman to be admitted in the history of Georgia.

At the time there were only four other Negro lawyers in Atlanta—probably less than a dozen throughout the state. The reasons for this were obvious: the courts are the main pillars of the jim-crow system. Negro oppression extended to literate Negro lawyers no less than to illiterate Negro sharecroppers. It made the role of a Negro lawyer fighting for justice a tragi-comic spectacle. If he dared to represent a white client—assuming that some such insane litigant could be found—he invited a lynching and the white client invited ostracism, if not worse, as a betrayer of white supremacy. No Negro lawyer wanted to submit himself to such a hazard to life and limb, unless, of course, he deliberately set out to challenge it. No Negro is more hated by Southern officialdom than an "uppity nigger," one who intelligently and firmly insists upon his constitutional rights. Punishment against him is swift and brutal.

The second reason for the scarcity of Negro lawyers is that the practice of law and all matters pertaining to the enforcement of the law is peculiarly a white-supremacy area. Negro businessmen and persons of means who could employ attorneys realized how handicapped they would be if they were defended by a Negro attorney against a white one in a court of law. Imagine a Negro attorney exposing some white attorney or white woman—Heaven forbid!—as a liar. It would no longer be a matter of legal procedure but a case of mob violence.

Thus Negroes were discouraged from employing their own attorneys except in petty cases, intra-Negro cases, or to draw up deeds, wills, contracts or other documents when there was not likely to be a clash with white attorneys.

I remember during my 'teens a litigation my father was involved in over the Odd Fellows—then the state's largest Negro fraternal society—in which several hundred thousands of dollars in property were at stake. My father had retained a former Atlanta judge as his attorney. I asked: "Why don't you get a Negro attorney to represent you?"

"Son," he replied, with amazement in his eyes, "the other side has employed a former state prosecuting attorney. Now where would I be getting a Negro lawyer to argue against him, to expose and denounce his arguments before a white judge. I might as well give up the ghost—even if I found a Negro lawyer with sufficient experience to handle such large matters."

"But, dad," I said, "You want me to be a lawyer. Wouldn't you have hired me?"

"Oh, that's different," he said optimistically. "I'm going to give you the best legal education you can get in the country. Besides, when you're ready to practice, things will be different."

At least in part, father kept his word. He sent me through one of the country's leading law schools. But he fell down on the other part of his promise—he was not able to change conditions. They are not too much different now than they were then. I still could not challenge the white supremacy system in the state of Georgia—and remain healthy—nor could I represent a white client, especially a white woman.

I hung out my shingle under circumstances that presented an interesting coincidence. My office, on the fifth floor of the famous Odd Fellows Building, had been my father's private office when he was District Grand Secretary of the Odd Fellows. The building at that time had already passed into the hands of the National Benefit Life Insurance Company—one of the bigger Negro national enterprises. It was a large and presentable office consisting of a waiting room and two private offices filled with high-grade furniture—stored there as the last material evidence of the once famous and wealthy Odd Fellows. I felt there was a certain fitness in my occupying my father's old suite.

After waiting a few weeks for throngs of clients to break down my door, one lone unsuspecting fly came into my parlor. It was a big moment. The case involved recovery from a small Negro insurance company for the death of my client's father, about

whose age at the time of contracting the policy there was some
question. My client was the beneficiary. Not more than $250 was
involved, although my zeal was as though it was $250,000.

I accepted the case and immediately called the company. I
spoke with the indignation that I felt—the company was trying
to avoid payment on the basis of a frivolous and unprincipled
technicality. I spoke as though I were a policeman, not a lawyer.
It was an outrage, I said, and they'd better "pay up or else." It
was my righteous indignation speaking. I quoted the company's
motto, "never missed a benefit," to the company representative
and accused the firm of hypocrisy; I told him it was a case of a
rich company stealing from a poor policy-holder. I almost
drowned the man in a torrent of words.

I was soon to learn, of course, that things weren't done that
way. Considerations of principle and equity didn't enter very far
into such negotiations. Next morning a young Negro attorney
came to my office. He had passed the bar a year ahead of me and
represented the company. I asked what case the company could
possibly have. It was clearly in the wrong and should pay up
and "that was that." If that was the way I felt about it, he
countered, then I should file suit. I replied there was nothing to
file suit over, since there was no question of principle involved.
He bade me good day.

I was at a loss to understand this. Nevertheless, I prepared to
sue, as much to punish the company as to recover my client's
benefits. But before suit was filed, the young attorney called me
for a luncheon appointment. We had lunch together and talked
the matter over. He was much wiser in the ways of the law than
I and he explained how such things were handled—out of his
year's experience, compared to my six weeks. We finally settled
out of court and my client received three quarters of the claim.
I could not, in good conscience, accept a fee, since I felt that the
full amount should have been recovered. The case, small as it
was, ate into my store of illusions.

The name of the young lawyer was John Geer. After our
luncheon, we struck up a fast friendship. As neither of us was

overwhelmed by clients, we had plenty of time to talk. Finally we decided to enter into partnership. Our firm became Geer and Davis.

My middle-class friends and associates were surprised at the partnership. Eyebrows were raised. It was considered a sort of betrayal of my class, since Geer was of poor working-class parentage, entirely unknown. He had had a sketchy schooling and had studied law on a self-study basis while employed as a menial worker. He was often half-starved, with a working wife and two kids to support. Just prior to passing the bar, he had been a bellhop in a local Atlanta hotel, where he narrowly escaped disaster. A few short months after he had left the hotel, the Negro bellhops in most of the largest hotels were rounded up by the police and charged with selling and running bootleg, soliciting prostitution, and the like. It was a big scandal that occupied the front pages for several days. As a matter of fact, the bellhops could not have held their jobs or made a living had they not made a fast buck on the side. Everyone knew this, including the judges and politicians behind the deal, for whom the bellhops has turned many a trick.

What was behind it? The answer came sharp and clear. All the Negro bellhops were replaced with white ones. The depression was on, and the bellhops who had held these jobs since the Civil War had to give their places to whites. It was the age-old tactic of playing Negro against white and white against Negro in the competition for jobs—only intensified by the economic crisis. And there was no trade union to protect any of them.

The newspapers raved in typical fashion: "Negro men involved in sordid traffic with white women, carrying on illicit relations . . . ." Lynch sentiment was deliberately incited against the Negro bellboys, spilling over onto the entire Negro population.

But one or two of the boys denounced the charges as a frame-up and threatened if the matter went to trial that they would name some of the Georgia bankers, preachers, legislators and other sanctimonious nabobs who had engaged their services. The matter quickly quieted down. But the Negro bellhops lost their jobs anyway. It was widely understood that in return for quietly withdrawing from their jobs, they would all be given light sentences or maybe probation—and that's the way it was.

Geer and I offered to defend these young fellows—most of them grown men with families, and they appreciated our offer. But they later decided that it was too great a risk to have Negro lawyers defend them.

I admired Geer's determination, his free and independent thinking, his consciousness of, and sensitivity to, the depressed conditions of the Negro masses. We had a division of labor in the firm: I took on matters of civil rights and corporate law; he occupied himself with negligence and insurance cases. We got along well—but not prosperously. Indeed, we could barely keep the wolf away from the door.

My first experience in court beyond the rail—the sacred fence that divides court officials from spectators—was an amusing if unhappy one, a sort of forecast of my future. In the midst of court session, I strolled inside the rail smoking a big black cigar. The chamber was jammed with spectators and officials. I took my seat behind the rail, not noticing the hushed silence that fell as I entered. Then snickers rose all around me. The judge, a tight-faced Ku Kluxer, rapped for order. I puffed away.

He pointed the gavel at me.

"Are you smoking a cigar?" he inquired, his face livid with rage.

"Yes," I replied.

He directed the bailiff: "Bring that man before me."

The bailiff, half-smiling, escorted me to the bench. My cigar was in my hand.

"What do you mean by smoking in court?" the judge asked.

"What's wrong with that?" I asked innocently.

"That's contempt of court," the judged replied hotly. "I fine you five dollars or five days in jail."

"I'm sorry. I didn't know. No offense was intended."

But the bailiff was already carting me off to the group of sentenced prisoners.

"Hold on," I said, resisting the bailiff's arm, "I'll pay it."

But as I searched my pockets I didn't have five dollars—only a couple of dollars and change. Whereupon, the court room roared.

Fortunately, Mr. Walden had come in during the incident. He handed me a five-dollar bill and I paid the fine.

Actually, I was so green I didn't know that smoking was prohibited in court. The morning newspapers had their fun, and so did pretty nearly everyone else. Even I laughed—a little later. I considered the incident closed. But I was wrong. When, in a subsequent case, I had challenged the custom of the court to call Negroes "nigger" or "darkey," at the same time defying the usual submissive demeanor required of a Negro attorney, the newspapers spoke of my arrogance, my "forgetfulness of the fact that the South was a white man's country," my impudent disturbing of peaceful relations between the races by challenging the time-honored jury system," and so forth. What was their evidence for this? That I had the cheek to disregard the customs of a court chamber by blowing cigar smoke in the judge's face in the midst of a judicial proceeding. . . .

The great depression struck Atlanta smack in the middle. Like a stone thrown into a pond, the blow hit the Negro population hardest, but the ripples spread to all other sections of the working people.

The most terrible result was mass unemployment. Negroes, traditionally the first fired and the last hired, constituted a disproportionate percentage of the jobless. Large textile mills were cutting back and throwing hundreds of thousands of white workers out of jobs, as well as the Negro workers who did the janitorial and other servile work about the factories. (They were barred from operating machinery or doing other skilled work.) Whites began to replace Negroes in jobs previously considered "Negro jobs"—chauffeuring, for example. Indeed, several chauffeurs who had been working with white families for many years were suddenly framed on charges of intimacies with female members of the family and driven out of the city.

Police brutality was on the increase, and incipient race riot situations became more frequent. In the rural sections, the semi-feudal lynch oppression of the Negro sharecroppers and tenant farmers had become so unbearable that the Negro section of the city swarmed with sharecroppers who had fled for their lives. My father and mother housed at least half a dozen of these hapless victims during that period. They were being hunted as the run-away slaves were hunted under the Fugitive Slave Law, before the Civil War. Our home was one of the first destinations of these victims, because my father was well known in the rural hinterland through his connection with the Odd Fellows and the *Atlanta Independent* as well as his leading position in the Republican Party. My father and mother had not forgotten the soil from which they came. Had any of these Negro fugitives been caught, they would have been returned to long stretches on a Georgia chain gang or to peonage, if not to certain death. They were accused of everything from "talking up to a plantation boss" to the "rape of a white woman." But, in every instance, their "crimes" were the result of the economic pinch which squeezed the countryside. Lynchings rose and fell with the price of King Cotton.

Negroes commonly lived in alley shacks without plumbing. Working-class areas were seething masses of discontent and ferment. This was true in white as well as Negro sections of the city.

This distressing condition reflected itself in Negro business, professional and middle-class circles. During this period, the Odd Fellows failed and lost its historic building. This blow affected almost the whole of Negro business and had a depressing effect upon the entire community. In addition, my father's paper failed—after 20 years without missing an issue. The collapse of the Odd Fellows, on which the *Atlanta Independent* was founded, made the bankruptcy of the paper inevitable. The white firm which printed the *Independent* teetered on the brink of failure for several months.

On the other hand, the Negro bank survived—with generous behind-the-scenes help from the white bankers to whom it had mortgaged its future. Certain Negro insurance companies reaped a harvest from the ruins of the less financially secure ones. And the wolf was so close to the door of several Negro institutions of higher learning that, under the skillful maneuvering of John Hope, president of Morehouse, Rockefeller interests were induced to buy control of almost all of them, consolidating Morehouse and Spelman colleges into a single university unit and liquidating Atlanta University as an undergraduate school. Thus did big business not only swallow its competitors during the economic crisis, it also gorged itself on bankrupt educational institutions—gaining complete domination over the largest Negro colleges in the deep South.

In the field of civil rights and equality before the law, the frame-up of the nine Scottsboro boys early in 1931 was the measure of justice to the Negro in the South. These youths—all in their teens—were bumming their way on a freight train in search of work to aid their poverty-stricken families. They were snatched from the freight and charged with raping two white girls, also hoboing in search of employment. They were quickly railroaded to a death sentence, which they narrowly escaped when the conscience of the nation was aroused by the efforts of the Communist Party and the International Labor Defense.

This, then, was the social and economic background against which I entered upon the practice of law. It contrasted rather sharply with the relative security that I had known as a middle-class person who possessed the necessary equipment for a moderately successful career—for a Negro, that is. Of course, I had learned certain positive lessons of struggle from my father and mother, and I had suffered painful, humiliating and sometimes threatening experiences as a Negro youth. These deeply rooted realities drew me closer to the fate of my people. On this mixed, patternless and somewhat contradictory background, my objectives began to take shape when I began my practice—and especially when I entered into the Herndon case.

CHAPTER FOUR

THE HERNDON CASE

In June 1932, I read in the Atlanta *Constitution* that Angelo Herndon, a 19-year-old Negro Communist youth, had been charged with "attempting to incite insurrection"—in violation of a Georgia statute which carried the death penalty. As originally passed in 1861 by the Georgia Legislature, the law was directed against slave insurrections, but was revised in 1871 to apply to both white and Negro "insurrections." A brief conference with my law partner, and I was off.

Herndon was imprisoned in the Fulton County Towers. I went there at once and, as an attorney, gained permission to interview him. We were locked into a cell on the first floor and had a "private" interview for about two hours (although the place was probably wired for sound). Here I learned, in brief, the story of Herndon's life and the facts upon which he had been indicted. I encountered no difficulties with the officials in securing that interview, although later I was to confront nothing but difficulties.

Angelo Herndon was born of a poor family with several children, and he had had to work to make ends meet for the family. He started in Alabama, where he ran into unemployment, oppression and jim-crow, piled on top of hunger. This brought him into contact with groups of older unemployed Negro workers and some white ones. He gravitated toward the unemployed councils, where he learned the value of organization and collective effort. His diligence, inquiring mind, precocity and militancy impressed his co-workers, and he soon became one of their leaders despite his youthfulness.

He read, and he studied, and he struggled. Eager to get to the bottom of things, he joined the Communist Party in Alabama. He became a leader in the party, as well as in the unemployed councils, and accepted a post as organizer in Atlanta. Here he assisted in the organization of a strong unemployed council— both Negro and white. As pay, he received seven to ten dollars a week—from time to time. When that wasn't forthcoming, he stayed with members of the organization and shared their pittance.

Their main slogan and objective was "jobs or relief." They put out sad-looking leaflets, collected nickels and dimes for their activities, held meetings and occasionally staged a demonstration in support of their demands. These demonstrations, starting out with eight or ten participants, soon grew into 50 or 60. Then they began to attract the attention of the city and state officials. The spectacle of Negro and white workers of the lowest economic level struggling together in comradeship and equality, defying segregation and white supremacy, was more than the Georgia jim-crow practitioners could take.

When, therefore, Herndon led an unemployed demonstration to the Fulton County Courthouse to demand bread, jobs and relief, he was arrested, and the anti-insurrection law, passed 66 years before and applying to an entirely different situation, was dug up to get Herndon. Actually, the real aim was to intimidate the people in the growing unemployed movement, to beat down their struggle against starvation and, above all, to stop what might one day drive the Southern plantation owners and lynch officials from power—the unity of Negro and white. Herndon had been selected as the target because, as in all such situations, the Negro is the most convenient scapegoat. He was indicted and held without bail.

I was greatly impressed by Herndon's story and demeanor and I offered at once to serve as council without fee. It was most shocking to me that a man could be put on trial for his life on the facts he had told me. I pledged then and there that I would move heaven and earth to secure his freedom and vindication.

Herndon then informed me that his defense was in the hands of the International Labor Defense, whose national headquarters were in New York City, and that he could not retain me without first advising with them. He would, he said, write to them and recommend that I be added to counsel—as he, too, had been favorably impressed with the interview.

My partner, Geer, and I met that evening on the case. We agreed to place our firm solidly behind the defense. Letters from Herndon and myself brought a representative of the national headquarters of the ILD to our office early in June. Our conference was wholly successful, and we reached agreement on all major points. The defense would be based upon the innocence of the defendant. The legal case would be based on the unconstitutionality of the Georgia insurrection statute, the exclusion of Negroes from the grand and petit juries, the right of citizens to assemble and petition their government against grievances. The case was to be defended by launching a vigorous counter-offensive against the white supremacy system upheld by the courts and by a campaign to uphold the legality of the unemployed councils and the Communist Party. In defending our client, we would unfold and expose the jim-crow conditions and the economic plight which gave rise to the militant Negro and white demonstration for which Herndon had been indicted. No other kind of defense could have been offered.

One hurdle still remained. The ILD had already employed an attorney—a white, Southern "liberal," at a fabulous fee. He had exploited the inability of the ILD to hire any lawyers at all in Georgia. The ILD was unofficially a "subversive" organization. This Southern white lawyer, who had no standing at the bar, could at the most arrange bail in certain labor cases and give a little legal advice here and there. But he would not fight on principle, since he was a white supremacist himself.

The ILD had fortunately retained an escape clause in its arrangement with him, and had not abandoned control of the litigation. When he was informed of the basis on which the ILD wanted the case defended, he withdrew, after throwing a fit— due, no doubt, to the sudden realization that his legalized blackmail of the ILD and his regular retainer were finished.

The coast was now clear. Nothing and no one could prevent a fighting defense of Herndon—which was to be a defense of the Negro people, the working class and American democracy.

My own qualms now entered the picture. I could see at once that it was no ordinary case—I sensed the elements of historic importance in it. But what disturbed me was the possible inadequacy of our firm to handle the case, and my own personal ability to measure up to what was required.

I talked this over with both Herndon and the national representatives of the ILD. I made it clear that I was no genius at the law, that my record in law school was far from distinguished. Further, I pointed out that I had been a member of the bar for only six months, that I had virtually no experience, and that indeed I'd never tried a case in court. I could not help feeling inadequate under the circumstances, and I knew that my conscience would never be clear unless I apprised both Herndon and the ILD of my shortcomings.

Both responded instantly that they not only wanted me to continue but that they wanted me to be chief trial counsel. I was a little taken aback by their positive decision, thinking that they should probably take a longer time to weigh the question. They liked my sincerity, fighting spirit, and my willingness to accept the responsibility. More than that, all of us had common cause in the conception that the issue of Angelo's freedom was the issue of Negro rights, of constitutional liberties. With this outlook on my part, they felt that the legal issues could be handled properly. Unless the working people of the country saw the basic issues involved and bestirred themselves in behalf of Herndon, the most expert and experienced legal talent would be unavailing—a truth which I was to learn a thousand times over. This, to me, was a qualitatively new approach to the judicial arena as the scene of struggle for democracy. It was at variance with everything I had learned at school and college. But a sympathetic chord was struck within me.

It was the real beginning of the interconnection between my personal desire for dignity and equal rights and the aspirations of the masses of my people for first-class citizenship. The oppression of the Negro people, the economic crisis and the Herndon case became one inseparable issue—and I was to be a symbol of that merger. A lot of things, hitherto unconnected, began to fall into place. A pattern was emerging. . . .

From June 1932, when we entered the case, until January 1933, when the trial took place, our firm devoted all its time to preparation of the Herndon defense. Everything else went by the board for me, although Geer struggled valiantly with little cases of one sort or another to keep our offices open and to pay the part-time secretary. In spite of this, he found time to assist in the Herndon preparations.

I had been out of law school for four years without practicing; I dug up all the old notebooks and texts I had used in law school, brushing up on all questions relevant to the case. I soon discovered, however, that the most important aspect of the preparation was constant consultation with my client, who was still in the Fulton County Towers.

A couple of weeks after we were retained, we moved for bail for Herndon. He was released on a $5,000 bond, which obtained until his conviction in January 1933. We offered him a place to live, decent clothing and a job as soon as he was released. But he declined all our assistance, saying, in effect, that his work was cut out for him and that he had "urgent business" with his comrades.

"What sort of business?" I inquired.

"I am still an organizer of the Communist Party," he said. "I've lost a lot of valuable time in jail. The key thing now is the organization of the unemployed and that's what I want to give my main time to."

"But I need you most of the time in preparing your defense."

"I'll be ready any time you want me. I'll get in touch with you every day, and you let me know when you want me."

This attitude was somewhat surprising to me. Here was a man on trial for his life, who, immediately upon his release from jail, wished to return to the very activities for which he was under indictment. He didn't want any commiseration even from his lawyer. He was right, of course; if his activities were perfectly legal and constitutional, why shouldn't he continue them?

After his release, he disappeared into the homes of his coworkers, who provided him with clothing, shelter and food. I did not inquire too closely, respecting his desires, believing that when he wished he would acquaint me with all details.

Soon enough we began daily consultations and preparations for the case. We held long conferences in my office, going over material, interviewing witnesses, outlining testimony and planning the defense.

I discovered that Herndon's first arrest had been illegal. He had been picked up at the post office when he went to get his mail at a PO box. When seized, all the material in his possession had been taken from him. The state police, who have no jurisdiction over federal property, had seized him and had confiscated his papers without a shred of authority. We secured a return of this material—mostly books, pamphlets, leaflets and old copies of the *Daily Worker*. The state officials, however, after releasing him from custody, arrested him at his home—this time legally. There they confiscated a number of leaflets, books and other educational material. Some of it pertained to the unemployed councils, others were Marxist classics and literature published by the U.S. Communist Party. The state based its case upon three of these pamphlets and an article in an issue of the *Daily Worker*. The pamphlets were: *The Communist Position on the Negro Question*, another on the lynch oppression of the Negro people, and a third, entitled *Communism and Christianism*—an attempt by Bishop William Montgomery Brown, retired, to relate Marxism to Christian ethics. The sum total of the bishop's reasoning was a favorable attitude toward communism and an attack on the hysteria against Communists incited by the reactionary leaders of the organized church—in which the bishop was *persona non grata*.

The article in the *Daily Worker* was entitled, "Everythng is Peaches Down in Georgia." I read this article a thousand times, and I could see nothing even remotely bearing on the case. It was a satire, citing the lynching, police brutality, peonage, unemployment, starvation and repression imposed upon the Negro and his poverty-stricken white fellow-Georgians. It was a lampoon on the Georgia Chamber of Commerce ballyhoo about Georgia as a peach state. By no stretch of the imagination could this article be held to be insurrectionary. At the most, it could be regarded as bad—if truthful—propaganda, too much for the thin-skinned white supremacists to take. But it was sufficient as one of the flimsy reeds upon which to hang a death sentence!

I not only read these four pieces of literature; I studied them diligently. In seeking to understand them thoroughly, I followed up all the references, going frequently to the classics by Marx, Engels, Lenin and Stalin. By the time the trial rolled around, I had a fair grasp of some of the basic theoretical principles of Marxism and of the program of the U.S. Communist Party. But this was only one part of my preparation. I considered it essential to learn about the practical side at first hand. I wanted to see for myself, and it was arranged that I should attend a few sessions of a Communist branch. One of the groups I met with was headed by a 60-year-old Negro iron worker, employed at an Atlanta foundry. Ten members were present—three white and seven Negro, men and women—meeting at the home of a Negro worker. (I never attended a single meeting that was not inter-racial.)

In this and subsequent meetings I found that the usual procedure was to discuss a major political issue, international or domestic, to make plans and proposals on local questions—unemployment, lynch terror, the Herndon case—pay dues (10¢ a month). They usually ended with refreshments. Occasionally classes in citizenship and in elementary reading and writing were held. (Later, after I myself became a member, I often taught these classes.)

Thus I witnessed a Communist branch in actual operation. I liked the experience so well that I never permitted a week to pass without attending a meeting. I enjoyed the society of these people even though they were cautious at first—until they felt sure that I was sincere and not a "plant" in lawyer's guise.

The final lap of my preparation had to do with defense witnesses.

January 1933 rolled around, and essentially the stage was all set for the trial. The newspapers had not published much about the coming trial, but what they had printed was vicious. There were rumors rumbling around that were hard to trace. Some of them had undoubtedly emanated from the white attorney who

had been withdrawn from the case. He resented his ouster and
set about making as many enemies as possible for the defense. A
few city big-wigs had tried to put pressure on my father by asking him how I happened to get into the case and what sort of
defense I was going to put up. He replied that he didn't know
very much about my intentions and figured that I was attracted
primarily by the novelty of the issue—and that I was young and
idealistic. The truth is, my father didn't know. Our defense plans
had been kept very much to ourselves.

The authorities and the ruling circles of the state had assumed,
I'm sure, that the defense would be the usual one where a Negro
has been charged with a capital crime and was to be defended by
a Negro attorney—that is, not only the defendant but also the
Negro attorney would throw themselves on the mercy of the
court. And while the defendant might get off with life or 30 years
—as long as his victim was another Negro and not white—both
the Negro defendant and his lawyer would have surrendered
something supremely valuable. They would have yielded to the
jim-crow system.

The state and court officials probably felt that this capitulation
would be all the more likely in our case, where the defendant
was "preaching" communism and, worse still, organizing poor
Negroes and whites together socially, economically and politically. They figured, too, I'm certain, that I would hew close to
the line of my father; that though I might show a few youthful
indiscretions as the outcome of my Northern education, I would
certainly realize that I had to live in Atlanta. In short, they were
not too disturbed and did not anticipate that the situation would
get out of hand.

But they were so wrong.

The preparation of our expert witnesses called for an exposi-
tion of revolutionary doctrine. One of these witnesses was Mercer
Evans, a professor of economics at Emory University—a leading
white university in Atlanta. He was brilliant, young, liberal in
his social outlook and courageous in publicly defending his views.
He had been attracted to the defense by the monstrous character
of the charge. For him to identify himself with the defense in

poll-tax, lynch-ridden Georgia was indeed an extraordinary exhibition of intestinal fortitude.

Professor Evans had organized and conducted a series of tests among his classes at Emory. One such test involved the selection of two passages that might be considered the most inflammatory writings of Lenin and Stalin; he then selected two passages from the writings and speeches of Lincoln and Jefferson. Without revealing the authors, he read these passages to his classes. He then asked which was the more revolutionary. In every instance, the students had chosen the passages from Lincoln and Jefferson.

Professor Evans, an excellent potential witness, normal in every respect, sprouting no horns, could not fail to make a strong impression. Similar tests had been conducted by Professor T. J. Conley, also of Emory, in other fields. The appearance of these two would in itself be revolutionary.

But while we intended a certain amount of humor in Professor Evans' testimony, we would drive home the point—that the American people had always had the right of revolution, whenever the majority of them saw fit to exercise it. How then could a man be indicted and convicted for upholding a right which was guaranteed by the Declaration of Independence and by our founding fathers?

Professor Conley was to testify on the economic essence of Marxism—that it involved, first of all, the transformation of the present capitalist system of economics into a socialist system of economics. Again, the point we would stress was: How could a man be tried for his life because he believed and advocated a system of economics that was different from the present system?

If the prosecution was right, the American colonists who were against the colonial system of economics—then dominated by the British Crown—and who advocated political and economic independence from Great Britain could be indicted under the Georgia insurrection stature. Such arguments would, we felt, lift the defense out of the area of refuting the slanderous accusations of "Negro domination," of the Negro's violence—sure to be dragged in by the prosecution and attributed to my client and his party.

As a matter of fact, a few weeks before the trial began, I had received a couple of warnings from the Klan, whose luxurious national headquarters was a tourists' showplace on Peachtree Street—referred to as such in much the same fashion as the many landmarks of the Confederacy. It was a tall, imposing, three-story, antebelleum house, plantation style, with the Ku Klux Klan flag waving in the Southern breezes, surrounded by odoriferous magnolia trees.

The Klan warnings I received, however, had none of this elegance. The anonymous telephone calls were from illiterates; the unsigned leaflets—always with the slogan, "The Klan Rides Again"—were so tattered and disreputable that one could only disregard them. But the crude attempts at intimidation were indicative of the mounting tension.

On January 16, 1933, when the trial began in the Fulton County Superior Court, the courtroom was packed with a mostly white audience. A few Negroes sat in the back, as if huddling together for protection against the glowering stares of the whites. Herndon, Geer and I sat at the counsel table to the right of the judge while the prosecution, with a battery of four lawyers, sat to the left of the judge, nearest the jury box. Inside the rail, the place was jammed with lawyers, occupying all the available chairs, with an even larger number standing around the sides, leaning on the judge's bench.

Naively enough, I had not suspected that this throng of people had come to witness the Herndon trial. But when I saw the last preliminary case disposed of, I noticed that no one moved. The stage had been carefully set by the presiding judge. This was obvious from the fact that in two of the preceding cases, the judge and prosecution had "bound over" two "bad niggers," one of whom was accused of assaulting a policeman. This sort of cruel and prejudiced procedure was so usual where Negro defendants were involved, that we could not altogether assume that it had been staged for our benefit; nevertheless, we exchanged understanding glances, like victims who had been shown the brutal fate awaiting us.

The judge was a humdinger. He was the Honorable Lee B. Wyatt of La Grange, Georgia, a backwoods town where a Negro lawyer would be as rare as a breath of freedom. He had been specially assigned to the Atlanta circuit for this case. None of the Atlanta judges wished to take it.

No doubt the Atlanta Superior Court judges were considered too sophisticated. They at least had seen Negro attorneys, few as they were, and did not regard them as no-tail bears. Atlanta, being a center of culture, naturally produced more "civilized" judges. Not so Wyatt. One might compare the strategy to that of a bullfight in which the most ferocious bulls are selected to challenge the matador. Here, the most ferocious judge was picked, so that the contrast between white supremacy and Negro servility would be sharpest. And it was expected that Herndon, Geer and I would be gored to death.

Wyatt fitted his role perfectly—as if he had been deliberately trained for years for this sole appearance in the judicial arena. He used the law with respect to Negroes like a butcher wielding a knife to kill a lamb. The man seemed astounded when, upon the calling of our case, I stood up to say: "The Defense is ready, your honor." He knew, of course, that I was the attorney; that was why he had been assigned to the case. But the reality overcame him—nothing had prepared him for what he was witnessing.

Upon the announcement of the clerk, the prosecution assistant solicitor-general, John Hudson, rose to say: "The State is ready, your honor."

If none of the resident Superior Court judges had wished to try the case, neither did John Boykin, solicitor general of Atlanta. An institution in himself, known for his rough-and-ready handling of Negroes, politically ambitious, he did not want to be mixed up with the hot tar of this case. Much to everyone's surprise, he assigned it to his chief assistant, Hudson, and his underling, J. Walter Le Craw, and their assistants. Boykin would give his assistants a chance to garner a name for themselves and to follow in his footsteps. He was in and out of the courtroom during the trial, an *ex officio* participant, making sure that developments went according to Hoyle, and conferring now and then with his hatchet men.

John Hudson was like a character out of a caricature. It was a coincidence that he combined the two attitudes deemed necessary to prosecute this case. Every day of the week he sent the little fry to the chain gang or to the gallows. On Sundays, he was also an ordained Methodist minister, and he was fully equipped to condemn the godless soul of a Communist to purgatory. If one of his talents didn't get you, the other would. Woe unto sinners and crooks! Hudson was one of the most consummate hypocrites—the only reason he wasn't a bigger one, as the jokester would say, is because he wasn't a bigger man. As a matter of fact, even physically he was generously proportioned—about six foot three and weighing about 200 pounds.

Le Craw was a small, chalk-white, wizened mummy of a man, as sorry in his appearance as he was in his actions. He was like a rubber ball, bouncing up and down with objections, exceptions, points of law—legal and illegal, irrelevant and what-not—all of which were sustained by Wyatt in his favor.

The first move of the defense was to quash the indictment as unconstitutional, null and void, on the grounds of the systematic exclusion of Negroes from the grand jury that indicted Herndon. We asked first that the court quash the indictment on its face, since it was admitted that no Negroes were members of, or had been called to, the jury. The court refused, instantly denying our motion. I asked to be heard in support of the motion. Judge Wyatt said:

"Heard? I just denied the motion. Nothing you'd say wouldn't make no difference, nohow."

I took an exception to this prejudicial and insulting comment.

We then moved to have testimony on the systematic exclusion of Negroes for the last 20 years or more. But the court banged the gavel:

"I told you, didn't I, that this indictment ain't going to be quashed on the basis of any motion you make?"

I arose and took an exception. I also took the occasion to remind the court that in all the precedents I had studied, no court had ever refused to hear evidence with reference to the factual operation of the jury system when that system was at issue.

But Judge Wyatt said: "Well, I ruled, didn't I? Move on to the next point."

This was out of this world. I looked at Geer, who was staring at me. The courtroom was as quiet as a mouse walking on cotton. The tension was unbearable. Obviously the judge was trying to convert every single point into a test of white supremacy practices. But I remained outwardly calm, though I boiled inside.

Knowing that the ruling of the court was reversible error, Prosecutor Hudson arose and declared that the state interposed no objections to the taking of factual evidence on the jury system. It was a direct hint to Judge Wyatt that he was going much too far. Indeed, the La Grange jurist had gotten himself way out on a limb, and, but for the intervention of the prosecution, would have sawed himself off.

"Proceed to the evidence," the judge announced in stentorian tones, as if he had never made his legally illiterate ruling.

We proved beyond a shadow of doubt that the jury system of Georgia in 1933 was illegal and unconstitutional, and had operated for 20 years in accordance with a policy of premeditated and deliberate exclusion of qualified Negro citizens. The evidence we adduced was not exhaustive, but it met adequately every test required by Supreme Court decisions to prove the illegality of the Herndon indictment and of the entire jury system.

We called a number of qualified Negro voters to the stand who had never been called for jury service. Among them was the late David T. Howard, the most successful Negro mortician in Atlanta, a very wealthy property holder and one of the prominent leaders of the community. He testified on direct examination that he had been a taxpayer for over 40 years, that he owned several thousand dollars worth of real property, that he voted in local elections, that he had no criminal record, that he was ready, willing and able to serve on both grand and petit juries—but that he had never been called nor had he ever received a jury summons in all these 40 years. Other equally qualified Negroes testified to the same thing. The point was solidly established.

Then we subpoenaed one of the State Jury Commissioners and put him on the stand. He was Steve Nance, a leader of the American Federation of Labor in Atlanta. He testified that the names of Negroes qualified for jury service were written on pink slips and the names of whites on white slips. When juries were selected, only white slips were drawn, pink slips deliberately discarded. This was to make certain, he pointed out, that no Negroes could possibly be drawn. He testified flatly: "No Negro has ever been called to serve on the Herndon grand jury or any other county jury during my tenure as a jury commissioner." Other commissioners, less cooperatively, nevertheless testified identically.

I then had the prosecutor, Mr. Hudson, take the stand in the face of the apoplectic glowering of Judge Wyatt, and he, too, testified that no Negro had ever been called during his score or more years as a county official. That sewed up the point. We rested. The prosecution placed no witnesses on the stand and did very little cross-examining. These preliminaries lasted only a day.

The court called for arguments, since no jury was present at this preliminary. A half-hour each was assigned for argument. Since I brought the charge, I had the opening and closing spots. But I gave the opening to the prosecution and took the last half-hour in one lump.

The prosecution took about ten minutes. It raised a number of technical points and finally declared that the jury system in Fulton County had existed for 50 years just as it was, that it was neither unlawful nor prejudiced, that it was in accordance with the judicial history and custom of the great state of Georgia, that it had meted out even-handed justice to both "Negra" and white defendants. "In all my practice of law in this honored court," said Hudson, flailing his arms like a windmill, "this is the first time that anyone dared to challenge our time-honored jury system."

At this point, I tittered.

The judge banged the gavel. He pointed its business end directly at me. "You'd better stop that snickering or I'll cite you for contempt."

I made no reply. How often I was to hear that threat later!

I pitched my argument in accordance with what I had learned at Harvard Law School. I told the court that here was one case in which the law and morality were clear and that I was confident that the court would enthusiastically welcome this rare opportunity to correct a historical and illegal wrong that violated all the highest judicial precedents, one that negated the rights of the entire Negro people. The facts were clear and we awaited his historic ruling.

The court chimed in: "It ain't clear to me."

Then I had Geer hand me three authorities and two decisions of the U.S. Supreme Court.

At this point, Judge Wyatt turned around in his swivel chair, so that his back was to me. I figured he was going to blow his nose and I waited until he wheeled around again. After I had waited a couple of minutes, the judge suddenly whirled about and told me I had ten minutes more.

"But I've hardly spoken ten minutes altogether," I said.

"You get ten minutes—that's all."

When I started to resume my argument, he turned his back to me again.

I spoke angrily: "Your conduct is unjudicial. I'm entitled to the same courtesy you extended to Mr. Hudson."

"That's enough from you," he shouted, pointing the gavel at me.

Two bailiffs closed in around me. The whole courtroom was tense. I ignored the threat and the insult and resumed my argument. I would speak until I was cut off by the judge or ejected.

"This case is so clear," I continued in a strong voice, "that even a layman could decide it without benefit of counsel. If, on the basis of the facts and the law governing this uncontradicted evidence, you do not grant a motion to quash this indictment, then I'll take you to the Supreme Court and reverse you."

I had spoken too boldly and committed, in legal parlance, an attempted threat upon the court.

Mr. Hudson was on his feet immediately.

"I object, your honor. That statement is contemptuous." Hudson was right, legally speaking. But the judge didn't know it.

Judge Wyatt, red in the face, told Hudson: "I'll handle this!" One would have thought that it was a question of which one of them was going to shoot me.

"Is that all you got to say?" he asked me.

Taking my good time, I replied, "Yes."

"Denied," he shouted and banged the gavel. "Court dismissed," he shouted again, banging the gavel continuously and getting to his feet.

For a moment I thought he'd gone berserk. He was beside himself with rage and stalked out of the courtroom, the gavel cocked in his hand as if he were going to brain the first person who got in his way.

"These people are stone crazy," I said. "This race prejudice is driving them mad. The Communists are right. Look at that judge!"

My "threat" to reverse Judge Wyatt had been quickly recognized as contempt by Hudson but he did not press it. It had been most offensive to the court, but the judge's reaction was unjudicially resentful. From his actions, it looked as though he wanted to fight. As it turned out, his stalking out of the court room had a more sinister meaning than was at first apparent. Although part of the packed audience had left, not interested in hearing the usually dry argumentation of counsel, the courtroom was still filled and there were still a few standees.

When Geer, Herndon and I walked through the rail and neared the door, we were surrounded by a group of murderous-looking white cutthroats.

"Watch yourself, or we'll string you up," one said to me. Another had an open knife in his hand. "Leave the Klan out of this," he said.

Still another: "We'll be here tomorrow and next day. That nigger red better be convicted."

There were seven or eight of these ruffians. We three walked slowly to the elevator, ignoring their threats, realizing that if we had replied in kind the odds against us would have been too great if violence had broken out.

Just then a courageous and steadfast friend appeared. "What's the trouble here?" he asked, sensing our situation. With him were two or three other Negroes.

Our nick-of-time friend was a well-known Negro minister, Rev. Martin, now deceased. A tall, strapping, well-built man with broad shoulders, copper-colored as an Indian, he weighed about 220 pounds, most of it muscle. He was about forty. I was to share many heroic and thrilling experiences with him.

"Davis," he said. "I have two or three members of my church here with me. We're going to escort you three to your office to make sure no harm comes to you." He spoke in a loud voice. Our would-be Klan assailants could hardly fail to hear him. They whispered to one another, broke ranks and slunk away.

Rev. Martin then showed us his revolver. "I expected something like this," he said. "So I brought this along with me, as well as three of my most loyal members. If they touched you fellows, we were going to let them have it. We watched you when court was dismissed and noticed when that bunch of lynchers started following you."

We took the elevator to the ground floor, and our friends walked us back to my office in the Odd Fellows building. When we arrived, Rev. Martin took charge. He gave me a lecture on the facts of life in Georgia.

"Davis, this is your home, just as it is mine, but you don't know what it's all about. Let me give you a few words of advice. Perhaps you don't realize it, but this case is historic. In all my life in Atlanta, I've never known the lily-white jury system to be challenged. The Klan elements in this town don't like it, and they'll resort to anything to stop it. Better be on your guard—I mean that literally. Ask your dad about these elements; he's encountered them many a time. I've been at his side. And now I'm going to be on your side for the rest of this case.

"These cracker elements don't frighten us; most of them are cowards. Most of them work directly with the police, who are just another arm of the Klan. I noticed that when court was dismissed all the court bailiffs and policemen hastily disappeared. They usually stand around until the courtroom and halls are cleared—especially if trouble is expected. I knew then something was up. The policemen were giving the Klansmen the right of way. If you had been attacked and beaten, the Ku Kluxers would have had time to do their damage and get away before the police got there to stop them and identify them. Besides, you wouldn't have been any better off if the policemen had come to your rescue.

"Davis, I know these Ku Kluxers as I know God's word. I have narrowly escaped lynching many times. Every time I did, it was because I chose to fight and die if necessary rather than submit. You see this scar on my face? Well, that came from being slashed by a Klansman who came to my house in South Georgia and tried to force me to take a ride with a Klan mob because I tried to teach our people to vote. He and two or three others came to my door, and when I refused to go with him, there was a scuffle and I was cut. My wife shot through the window. I closed the front door and shot at them, wounding two. Before they could get back with a mob, my wife and I escaped to Atlanta—where we've been ever since. During the riot in Atlanta I used my church as a fort.

"So you see, be prepared for anything; be ready to protect yourself. And fight this case to the limit of your constitutional rights. This is what we need in Atlanta, although a lot of my kind of Negroes are afraid to say so. You go right ahead. The man on the street is with you, and he's the one who'll fight."

I was warmed by the minister's little talk. "I'm sure proud of and grateful for your interest." I spoke for Geer and Herndon as well.

He said: "I don't know anything at all about communism. I've heard about the Scottsboro case, how the Communists kept the Alabama authorities from summarily executing those nine boys. But if communism has anything to do with what you're doing in this case for the freedom of my people, I'm with you one hundred per cent.

"Now, I tell you what I'm going to do. I'm going to meet you three in front of the courthouse every morning of this trial, 15 minutes before court convenes. With me will be my two friends. Every day we're going to escort you to and from lunch and back to your office in the Negro neighborhood after court. I'm going to sit inside the rail with you during the trial."

"That won't be necessary," I said. "But just the same, thanks. It's our cross and we'll bear it. We don't want you to endanger yourself in any way on our account. I'll never forget this offer, though."

"Davis, this is the cross of the whole Negro population of Atlanta. It ought to be the cross of every white man with any Christianity or justice in his soul. But we're going to be with you just the same. That's final. See you in the morning."

He got his hat and left, taking his friends with him.

Herndon, Geer and I glowed. I thought to myself: "There's no end to the heroism of the Negro people."

The next morning was to mark the beginning of the substance of the case. Preceding the actual trial there had to be the selection of a jury.

Just before I left home for the office, a stranger's calling card greeted me. As I walked out of the front door to my car, there was a white cross stuck into the lawn. It was about four feet high with a two-foot cross bar. It was wrapped in white material, and on the front of it, facing the street, was a Klan leaflet with the words: "The Klan Rides Again. Get out of the Herndon case. This is a white man's country." The leaflet was decorated with three white-hooded Klansmen riding horses and holding flaming torches high above their heads.

I called my father. He came out, looked at it and said: "Son, I've seen so many of these that they don't frighten me any more."

I pulled the cross out of the ground and took it back into the house to keep as a memento. And then I left for court. Geer, Herndon and I met Rev. Martin and his party on schedule. When we got to the courtroom, we had to get the assistance of the bailiff to get in—so packed were the chamber and hallway.

Rev. Martin entered within the rail with us while his two friends made their way to the jim-crow section at the back of the court. The plan was so well organized that friends had saved a couple of seats for them.

How Rev. Martin remained inside the rail, boldly sitting at our counsel table, is as much a mystery now as it was then. Perhaps they thought he was part of counsel—it would be un-imaginable to the court that I would be so impertinent as to violate this sacred part of the chamber. Or perhaps it was because he was a minister (Negro ministers usually enjoyed certain privileges), and they considered it disrespectful to ask him to leave. The selection of the jury began.

The prospective jurors had been well drilled. Their answers were so cut-and-dried that I decided to tackle a couple. I questioned one who had made a particularly slick and routine reply: "In support of your oath to tell the truth, tell the court whether you're a member of the Ku Klux Klan."

Surprised at this direct thrust, he answered: " I am but that wouldn't prevent me from giving a fair verdict."

A spontaneous howl of laughter spread over the courtroom, starting apparently from the Negroes in the jim-crow section.

Judge Wyatt banged the gavel: "Order in this court. The next time I hear any laughter, I'm going to clear the rear benches." In my naiveté, I wondered how he would dare exclude the Negroes and leave the whites. But as the trial progressed, I would not really have been surprised at that—not from Judge Wyatt.

When order had been restored, I rose and asked the court to strike the juror for cause. Judge Wyatt, who even for appearance's sake should have instantly granted the motion, showed his determination to grant no motion of mine—law or no law.

"Well, I don't know about that," he said pontifically.

I looked in amazement. Here was an acknowledged member of the Klan and the judge pondered whether he shouldn't be a member of the jury! At various points during colloquies with the court, I had all but exploded. This time, and on the issue, I was going to shoot the works, confident that the court's refusal to strike a member of the Ku Klux Klan for cause was reversible error.

But Prosecutor Hudson rose and declared: "Your Honor, the state interposes no objection to the striking of this juror for cause. But without prejudice to the integrity of the juror and to the reputation of any organization he wishes to join."

Thus the prosecutor, compelled by the issues and public sentiment involved, granted my request. But at the same time, he let the world know that the Klan was a respected organization against

which the state officials harbored no animosity or ill will. . . .
After a few more tilts with the judge and prosecutor, the jury
was finally chosen by the end of the day.

The next day, the prosecution called on its first witness, an
assistant prosecuting attorney, who gave the facts as to the arrest
and literature seized. It was from Stephens that Hudson elicited
the lurid tales of "Negro domination" based upon the pamphlet
entitled, *The Communist Position on the Negro Question.* In the
course of his testimony, Stephens referred to Herndon as that
"nigger" sitting there, pointing at him.

I jumped angrily to my feet. "I object, your Honor. The term
'nigger' is objectionable, prejudicial and insulting."

The Court: "I don't know whether it is or not."

"Your Honor, your remark made before this jury that you
don't know whether it is or not entitles my client to a mistrial.
I move a mistrial."

"Motion denied," he said, hardly waiting for me to finish my
sentence.

Again, I rose: "Your Honor's remark is not a ruling. I insist
upon a ruling by the court."

"That's all the ruling you're going to get."

"Exception," I countered.

"However," he continued, "I'll instruct the witness to call him
'darky,' which is a term of endearment."

"Exception. What's more, the term is equally offensive and
prejudicial. I renew my motion for a mistrial."

"Denied."

The bulk of the prosecution's case was presented in the testimony of the assistant district attorney—a government employee.
The state had not found a single stoolpigeon. It is to the credit
of the staunch white and Negro workers that not one of them
would serve as a rat for the Ku Klux prosecutors.

Later the same day, we presented our case. Our witnesses were
Professors Evans and Conley, one county official and Angelo
Herndon. Our attempt to validate the testimony of the professors
was a tragi-comedy. On direct examination, Professor Evans gave
his qualifications as an expert on communism, and described it

as essentially a social system based upon economics for use instead of for profit.

But the judge—completely out of his depth and unable to go beyond his Klan-level mentality—arbitrarily refused to qualify him. And the jumping-jack flunkey Le Craw bobbed up and down with captious objections, openly steering the court.

At one point I asked Professor Evans: "Basically a communist social system is a system of economics, isn't it?"

"I rule that question out of order," interrupted Judge Wyatt. And then, to my astonishment, he went on: "The state is not trying to prove that Herndon is not an economical man."

"Your Honor, who said it was? What has that got to do with this case—whether the defendant is economical or extravagant?"

The gavel came down with a thud. "That line of questioning is ended. I've ruled. I'm running this court."

Prosecutor Hudson asked a few stupid, lynch-inciting questions on cross-examination—all of which Professor Evans deftly turned against him.

Professor Conley was put through the same wringer by the court and the prosecutor, with the court doing more prosecuting than the prosecutor, who did everything possible to turn the trial into a challenge to white supremacy. Naturally the jury was supposed to react to this with fire and brimstone.

He asked Professor Conley: "Would you want your daughter to marry a negra?"

I objected vehemently. "Overruled," said the court, like a phonograph record.

Professor Conley replied: "I have no daughter."

"Would you want your sister to marry a negra?"

"I object, your Honor, in the strongest terms."

"Overruled," the judge droned monotonously. "Answer the question."

"I have no sister," he replied.

"Would you want any of your women kinfolk to marry a negra?" He wasn't going to be cheated of this question.

I got up out of my chair, but before I could say anything, Judge Wyatt banged the gavel: "Overruled."

Professor Conley calmly and thoughtfully said: "It makes no difference what I want. It's against the law of this state for Negroes and whites to intermarry. I would not advise nor want anyone to do anything to break the laws of this state."

Then I called to the stand jailor Holland, superintendent of the Fulton County Towers, where Herndon has been incarcerated. It was my purpose to prove out of his own mouth the brutal mistreatment of my client. He was, of course, most uncooperative—surly, vicious, arrogant, consumed with hatred of Negroes. He preferred the rope and faggot—was intolerant of even this farce of a trial. . . .

Our last witness was the defendant. Under the laws of Georgia a defendant could make only an unsworn statement on the stand and was immune from both direct and cross examination. Herndon kept the courtroom enthralled for 35 minutes, uttering the now famous words:

"No matter what you do with this Angelo Herndon, thousands more will arise to take his place, to fight the battles of the Negro people and the workers until they are free."

To the Negro people in that courtroom, and for the oppressed, colored and white, all over the world, these words gave inspiration and strength. I felt an inner glow at hearing them—an earnest of the fact that here indeed was a new force at work for the liberation of the Negro and for human betterment.

This was the climax of the trial. It had arrayed the world of white supremacy and racial hatred against the forces of freedom and dignity.

Later that evening, I turned over to my client my application to become a member of the Communist Party.

My association and experience with the Communists and the study of Marxism incidental to my preparation for the defense (as well as my own victimization as a Negro by the jim-crow system) resulted in that decision. I was, at 29 years old, sure of the Marxist outlook as the path of liberation for the Negro people, the path that would lead to the betterment of the entire American people. At last I was able to counterpose to my father a solution of the struggle that he had engaged in for 50 years of his life without getting nearer to first-class citizenship. What I had not found at Morehouse, Amherst and Harvard I had discovered in a dingy Georgia courtroom whose realities were far more penetrating than the abstractions of classical scholarship.

It was a grim joke on Judge Wyatt, not to mention Reverend Prosecutor Hudson. Their fulminations were designed to fill the Negro, first of all, and then the poor whites, with the "fear of God." They were supposedly demonstrating that the wages of Communist adherence is relentless persecution. . . .

The final day of the trial brought argument of counsel, the charge of the court and the verdict of the jury.

The court permitted two hours each to defense and prosecution, with the latter having the right to close. The prosecution divided its time—Prosecutor Hudson speaking the first hour, defense taking the next two hours, and Le Craw taking the last hour.

Hudson made a speech in defense of white supremacy against the "Godless assault of communism and Negro domination." His inflammatory remarks—to which I objected and excepted until I was weary—amounted to a verbal lynching of the Negro people. He flailed his arms, preached, snorted, read excerpts from the forbidden pamphlets, pounded the jury box, pointed his forefinger at Herndon, quoted the Bible, painted a picture of threatened virginal white womanhood, swayed his body left and right as if he were trying to hypnotize the jury—appealing to them to do their duty by sending this "black viper to the electric chair."

I was fascinated by the antics of this soul-saving Ku Kluxer. At the same time, I was delighted by the private knowledge that whereas the day before he spoke to one Communist, today he was speaking to two. He had no one but himself and his kind to blame.

Geer and I had agreed that he would speak first one hour and I would follow immediately for the second hour. Geer spoke 15 minutes. I had hardly glanced over my brief pencilled notes before I was compelled to start my address. I began in the heat of anger:

"Ladies and gentlemen of the jury:

"Don't become hungry. Don't use your constitutional right to petition your government against grievances. Don't come to the courthouse seeking bread for your children. Don't become unemployed. Don't regard your Negro neighbor as a fellow-sufferer and join with him to improve your lot. If you do any of these human, legal things, you're attempting to incite insurrection and Mr. Hudson will send you to the electric chair.

"Mr. Hudson is a very Christian-like gentleman. Five days a week in this courtroom he sends hapless Negroes and innocent poor whites to the electric chair. But on Sundays he's all milk and honey. He's an ordained minister and he preaches to the people the doctrine of mercy to the poor and unfortunate. He gets forgiveness for his own crimes of the preceding five days a week. Such hypocrisy! This is the hypocrite who wants you to take the life of my client. In fact, he assumes that this will be an easy task. After all, my client is only a young Negro. He relies upon the prejudice and hatred of Negroes to guarantee the fearsome words from your mouths that will send my client to the electric chair.

"Far from sending this 19-year-old Negro youth to the electric chair, he should be hailed for his courage, for the obvious common sense of his mission. He was getting together the poor of both races, unemployed through no fault of their own, to work in unity and brotherhood to fight hunger. This has long needed to be done in this, of all states in the South—where too long the poor Negro and poor white have been rent apart, to the detriment of both. Mr. Hudson, yes, the state of Georgia, should welcome interracial brotherhood. That is only Christian. It should appeal to Mr. Hudson. Instead, he wants to send the advocate of this brotherhood—who dared to bring it about—to the electric chair. Mr. Hudson's vaunted piety is only a cloak for his evil deeds. Does he believe in brotherhood or does he believe in human hatred and division?"

I turned to Reverend Prosecutor Hudson:

"Which is it, Mr. Reverend-Prosecutor? Why don't you tell the jury?"

By this time, some members of the jury were in such a rage at me that they could not conceal it. In order to keep my composure, I had walked slowly in front of the jury box from one end to the other, speaking in a well-modulated tone of voice, rising occasionally to a crescendo to emphasize a point. But the jurors in the front row were turning their backs to me as I walked in front of them.

I continued my attack on Hudson:

"Mr. Hudson read to you from pamphlets on communism. He knows nothing of the subject, and moreover does not wish you to have any enlightenment, or else he would not have objected to the qualifications of Professors Evans and Conley as expert witnesses. Mr. Hudson knows as much about communism as a pig knows about a full-dress suit. I'll read to you certain passages from these pamphlets in evidence which Mr. Hudson conveniently forgot."

For a half-hour I read to the jury from the pamphlet detailing the oppression of the Negro people in the United States—particularly in the deep South and in Georgia. One passage contained a vivid and terrifying description of the bestial lynching of a pregnant Negro woman. This helpless woman was burned at the stake by an infuriated white mob.

At my reading of those passages, a hush fell on the courtroom. My voice was hoarse from the sustained strain and indignation under which I had been speaking. A whisper gave my voice an even greater melancholy and pathos. As I finished, a woman in the audience screamed and fainted—a white woman.

I asked for a moment's recess, but the court denied it. I wanted to rest my failing voice, also to permit the dramatic passage I had just read to sink into the conscience—if any—of that hostile jury.

I resumed my argument with only a few minutes to go, rummaging through the pamphlets, picking and choosing among passages which I had marked. I exhibited pictures from the material, most of them showing a Negro and white worker or sharecropper shaking hands. I asked the bailiff to pass them among the jury. Some of the jurors refused to look at them.

Then I asked: "Mr. Hudson accuses my client of stirring racial hatred. Do you see one illustration of antagonism or hatred among them? . . . Do you see the symbols of hatred and oppression such as exist on the materials of the Ku Klux Klan? Where is the 'insurrection' that the state charges?"

I went over the evidence, denouncing the fact that while the prosecution had charged my client with attempting to incite insurrection, he had produced not a single witness who testified to a single act of violence or insurrection committed by my client. "Would you call a peaceful demonstration for relief an attempt at insurrection? If a man has a hungry baby, is he attempting to overthrow the government if he, in concert with his neighbors, petitions the government officials for assistance? . . . Even the assistant prosecutor couldn't find any insurrection. All he could find was an innocent 19-year-old Negro youth who had in his possession pamphlets which the prosecutor didn't like. . . .

"Mr. Hudson strongly dislikes the slogan of self-determination for the Black Belt. He bellowed and howled over it, but not once did he explain it to you. . . . Permit me a few words on it: The Black Belt is an area in which the Negroes are a majority, large enough in some states, as in Mississippi, to contain more Negroes than whites. By every principle of democracy, the Negroes should be governors, mayors, congressmen, senators, local and county officials. What is insurrectionary or revolutionary about that? It is simply majority rule under the traditions and principles of both the federal and state constitutions. . . .

"But Mr. Hudson violently objects. Why? It is not difficult to fathom. Once the Negro majority has the right to vote, to elect its own officials, to secure schools, to secure justice in the courts, to earn a decent living, it means curtains for the lynchers, the poll-taxers, the Ku-Kluxers, the white supremacists. It means the enforcement of the 13th, 14th, 15th amendments to the U.S. Constitution. . . . It means a Southland for, of and by the people —instead of for, of and by the mill owners, landlords and corrupt officials."

As I closed, I looked intently at the jury. It was no use. There wasn't a reasonable countenance among them; for the most part, their faces were twisted in anger, hostility and rage.

The last hour of argument was assigned to Mr. Le Craw. This legalistic jumping bean detailed the tenderness that the "white people had for the negra even during slavery. We've been looking out for them, taking them into our homes, allowing them to rear our children. Is there greater consideration for negras than that? Are we going to permit these godless red Communists, masked behind the face of this black negra boy to tell us how to run our states, our courts and our lives? Was there ever a more sinister challenge to law and order, to Christianity, to the benevolent rule of the white man?

"The lawyer for this boy says the only thing he did was to possess these books and lead a demonstration. Do we have to wait until they get their Red 'Rooshian' army together to attack our homes, take our property, rape our women, and murder our children? Do we have to sit until they perfect their schemes of insurrection and violence?

"Let's put this thing down now. Let's throw the fear of God into all who come into our fair state of Georgia to preach their blasphemous doctrines of equality. . . . Let's make the troublemakers and agitators quiver in their boots. The electric chair is too good for those who would rape our women. We have been good to the negras. They are our wards."

At this point I was on my feet demanding a mistrial.

"A mistrial? What for?" glowered Judge Wyatt.

"Prosecution referred to Negroes as wards of the state. Negroes are citizens, not wards. This reference is erroneous, misleading and highly prejudicial. No instruction of the court can erase this vicious insinuation from the jury's mind."

"Denied. Don't you dare interrupt the argument of counsel again. The next time it's contempt of court."

"Exception to the use of the term 'ward,' and to the remarks of the court," I said, in controlled anger.

"Take all the exceptions you want," he said contemptuously.

"Exception to that remark, your Honor," I said, trying to express my bitter personal anger in legal terms.

Le Craw raved for an hour and sat down. The court's charge to the jury was clearly a directed verdict of guilty. It was a strain on the imagination to regard it as a charge to the jury. I excepted to each and every paragraph of his instructions. After he had finished, I expected the jury to stand instantly in the box and shout 'guilty,' or even to physically assault my client.

I was amazed when the jury took three hours to arrive at a verdict. "Have you arrived at a verdict?" the court inquired. "We have, your Honor," said the foreman. "What is it?" "We, the jury, find the defendant guilty—with a recommendation of mercy."

I knew what that meant—20 years on a Georgia chain gang. A living death! There was a sigh in the courtroom. I made two motions—one to set aside the verdict, the other to continue my client's bail. Both were summarily denied.

The bailiffs latched vigorously on to Herndon's arms and practically shoved him out of the courtroom.

I grabbed his hand. We looked at each other with understanding. I assured him of an immediate appeal.

As for me, I had entered the trial as his lawyer and ended it as his Communist comrade.

CHAPTER FIVE

AFTER THE HERNDON TRIAL

Soon after Herndon's conviction, the offers of help and solidarity from Atlantans flowed into my office, most of them from Negroes, but not all. The two points most stressed in these messages were the case as a symbol of the inequality of the Negro before the law and the violation of the right of free speech.

These friendly messages were a mandate for action. I sent out an invitation to a small group of the people who had written us—a cross-section of the population—and asked them to come to my office. A group of about 25 people came—among them workers, students, church people, intellectuals, social workers and business people. We had a lively session and a very practical one. Some held tenaciously to their opposition to communism but felt that the cause of justice for the Negro went beyond political labels or religious creed.

The result of this meeting was the organization of the Provisional Non-Partisan Committee for the Freedom of Angelo Herndon. It set itself the task of holding a larger-scale conference, of inviting all kinds of organizations to send representatives and mapping a program of action.

The police department, however, also got busy. Several members of the original committee found themselves the object of attention from the police, who asked: Did Mr. or Mrs. So-and-So know that Communists were behind the Herndon case? Were their names used with their consent? Negroes were asked whether they knew that Communists were stirring up racial strife. Whites were asked did they want their daughters to marry a "nigger"? These questions constituted a clear attempt to intimidate the participants and smash the conference. But the committee stood solid.

Actually, the police department had unwittingly contributed

to the success of the conference. Almost a thousand people attended—a good cross-section of the people, with a number of professionals and prominent leaders present. Herndon spoke of his case and its significance to the workers, giving the community for the first time a vivid presentation of the Communist approach to the struggles of the Negro people against the lynch system.

The upshot of the conference was the establishment of a committee for Herndon's defense, the adoption of a program of action, and the raising of funds. Most important of all, it was the first conference of its type ever held in Atlanta. And out of the conference, there arose a movement. All over the city various types of action were initiated. Churches passed resolutions, ministers preached sermons; fraternal societies took a stand; young people and college students became active campaigners for the issues.

The case took on a national and international character. Progressive people all over the world sent greetings, issued statements, visited American consulates and embassies with protests. The Negro press took up the case nationally and condemned the conviction as an example of jim-crow justice in the deep South. But, above all, the organized labor movement took up the case. Large numbers of trade unions passed resolutions—even though many of them expressed their disagreement with the policies of the Communist Party.

AFL unions which expressed support did so in the face of bitter red-baiting by William Green and the reactionary top leadership. In fact, the AFL's failure to take a stand for Negro equality in cases of this sort was one of the prime reasons for the subsequent organization of the CIO in 1935. Nevertheless, a certain sympathy for the Negro rights issue, especially on the question of unemployment relief, was stirred among the rank and file AFL workers in Atlanta, where the labor movement was practically entirely white. It was because of this that Steve Nance, an AFL leader and one of the jury commissioners who had testified in the Herndon case, gave permission for the Herndon Defense Committee to meet in the AFL labor temple.

The defense movement became a people's movement and began

to express itself on other issues as well. At that time police brutality was at its peak. Many Negro leaders—church and college leaders especially—had protested, but to no avail. One day Glover Davis, a blind Negro, was shot to death by the police. They had gone into his home to arrest him, a bitter argument ensued, and he was killed. Glover Davis was well known and liked throughout the Negro community, and there was widespread resentment. Sensing the situation, instead of taking action against the guilty cop the police department posted a large force near the Odd Fellows Building, making it look like an armed camp.

A group of citizens came to my office for assistance. The Herndon Defense Committee decided to have a mass funeral, and a church was finally secured despite police intimidation of the ministers. The church, which held about a thousand people, was jammed, and fully another thousand milled around outside. There were at least 200 police present, including several higher officers, with 50 posted inside, their night sticks in plain evidence. The cops delayed the ceremony for a full hour and a half trying to persuade the minister to "use his better judgment" and call it off. The minister stood his ground, and the funeral proceeded.

Inside the church, nerves were taut but the people did not budge. Neither did the crowd outside. Along the streets in the block surrounding the church, police were stationed in battle formation, guns and tear gas equipment prominently displayed. On the roofs of adjacent buildings guns were mounted. Thanks to the discipline of the Negro working people in that tense crowd the police provocation proved unsuccessful.

The funeral went off as scheduled. It was in part religious, in part secular. First, the minister delivered a short eulogy and sermon, followed by hymns and prayers. Afterwards, the Citizens Committee took over. Both white and Negro workers spoke, and the tension in the church became even greater. The audience sensed that this is what the police had tried to prevent. One white woman, a mill worker from the Fulton Bag & Mill Company, spoke with deep feeling. Although she was no finished elocutionist, she manged to convey in homely language that not all white

workers were racists and that many of them were beginning to
realize that they must stand together with the Negro to save
themselves. The audience greeted her brief, heartfelt words with
a chorus of sighs and "Amens."

In my own remarks I said that the funeral expresses the mass
sentiment of the Negro community and of their white friends
against police brutality, and that we would not be intimidated
by the show of police power. I urged everyone to write a personal
letter to the Mayor condemning the murder of Davis and calling
for an end to police terror. My remarks were exceedingly mild.
Nevertheless, one of the police officials lingered after the services
to tell me: "I will see that you are held personally responsible for
any disorder that results from this meeting. We're not going to
tolerate any Communist uprisings by niggers in Atlanta. This is
a white man's country and the quicker you learn that the better."
I disregarded him and started to walk away when the police attempted to secure the names and addresses of my friends standing
by. I promptly protested, knowing that they would be put on job
blacklists. "As their counsel," I told the police, "I will take
personal responsibility for their failure to reveal their names and
addresses." In a huff, the policeman walked away, saying, "You'll
hear about this," but I never did.

The ILD, which did not have a branch in Atlanta prior to the
Herndon case, now had an office where people came to express
their support and to participate in activities. It attracted more
than a hundred members, both Negro and white, in a short
while. I was elected as its branch attorney. It held meetings,
concerts and rallies devoted to the defense of the Negro people
from jim-crow oppression; it took up the issues of the white
workers as well; and its great strength was its Negro-white membership and unity on a basis of equality. Hardly any case of
police brutality took place without the victims calling in the
ILD. It turned the spotlight of publicity on numerous anti-
Negro injustices which otherwise would have gone unnoticed in
the dark of the moon.

This was all too good to be true. The city officials set the police
on the organization; visits were made to officers of the branch;

Ku Klux messages repeatedly came to the offices. Finally, a series of raids were made on the ILD offices. They took place in the dead of night. But they found nothing but leaflets, literature, publications of various types. Not even this hooliganism stopped the organization.

The raids now started in broad daylight. I was present during one of them, along with a Negro officer of the branch and the young white woman secretary.

Three policemen burst in, led by none other than the assistant solicitor, John Hudson, in person. They demanded the names of all present and proceeded to search the premises. They found nothing but an old battered desk, a couple of chairs and a box of leaflets. I demanded a search warrant, but Hudson was ready for me. He then took a seat and began to question the secretary. By that time the place was a shambles—papers and drawers littering the floor.

I intervened to advise the secretary to answer no questions. Hudson looked at me in a rage. "Keep your mouth out of this," he bellowed.

I then advised the lady to leave the premises and go home. "You'll not get out of here," Hudson said sharply, as the police barred the door.

"You've found no commission of a crime here that entitles you to arrest or hold anyone in protective custody."

"Shut up," Hudson said.

"I'm the attorney for this organization."

"You may be attorney for this organization. But you're not attorney for this—this white woman," he said, as if he were putting the finishing touches on me.

The young lady spoke up: "He is my personal attorney."

"What!" he shouted. "You want a negra for a lawyer!"

"He's my attorney and I'm going to follow his advice," she said firmly. "I won't answer any of your questions."

Hudson nearly burst a blood vessel. "That don't happen here," he said, and he stalked out of the office.

I was as much amazed as Hudson. Here was a mere slip of a girl—a Southern white girl, born in the mountains of Georgia, in one of the most backward sections, in a virtual center of moonshine manufacturing where policemen and angels feared to tread. Her family were poor hillbillies. She could not have come from a more prejudiced background. Negroes who wandered into the neck of the woods where she lived just disappeared. What she had done was to interpose her own reputation and character between a group of lynch officials and me. Thereafter, she was a marked woman. White women in Georgia didn't do things like that and get away with it.

"Why did you do that?" I asked.

"I don't know. I was as mad as I could be. I never saw a white man treat a white woman as badly as he was treating me. I expected him to be nasty to you, but I didn't expect him to talk to me as if I were a dog."

"Yes, but you didn't have to make me your personal lawyer. It will make the white supremacists see red."

"I thought of that. But he was being nasty to me and you were protecting me. So that made you my lawyer anyway."

This was the first time I had represented a white client. I left word at Hudson's office that any time he wished to pursue the question of the raid further, he could notify me, as I would represent the ILD secretary as her personal attorney—as well as representing the organization. I heard no more of this. Later we recovered the literature that Hudson's police had carted out. . . .

The Herndon case had become a big issue far beyond the banks of the Chattahoochee River. Every angle of the case became a matter of public interest. Several months of prison confinement in the Fulton County Towers had played havoc with Herndon's health. His weight went down sharply, and he was plagued with stomach trouble from the poor jail food. Finally I became alarmed. I sent word to the ILD national office in New York, and they in turn reached scores of organizations and friends. Hundreds of protests rained in on the Georgia state officials; liberal publications in the North which had condemned his conviction joined in the protests. Many flatly charged that the jail officials were trying to do away with the defendant before he had had an opportunity to submit his case to appeal. The spotlight was focused on the brutal Georgia prison system.

Finally, a delegation was formed in the North to come to Atlanta on the issue of Herndon's health. They demanded medical attention for the prisoner from his private physician. Prior to their arrival, however, the state prison commissioner issued a statement declaring that Herndon was in perfect health, was receiving expert medical attention, and that the hue and cry about his mistreatment was "a communist plot engineered by Yankee meddlers."

But the delegation came anyway—eight of them, with two Southerners among them—a white woman and a white man. I took them to Hudson's office to get a permit to visit Herndon. He was rude and insulting.

"Hell, you'll get no permit from me. You're nothing but a bunch of Yankee meddlers and troublemakers interfering with the processes of justice in this state. All of you get out of my office."

"Your treatment of these visitors from sister states is disgraceful and reveals the truth of their accusations," I said. "I shall protest this matter to the governor."

The delegation repaired to my office. I called the governor's office and informed his secretary of Hudson's treatment. He said he would call me back, and he did in about 15 minutes. The governor, Eugene Talmadge, would see the delegation the next morning at 10 AM.

The delegation decided to invite Rev. Martin to come along, and he was happy to do so.

As the delegation filed in, Talmadge, in short sleeves and galluses, shook their hands. Rev. Martin and I were last. He didn't shake our hands. He asked: "You boys with them?"

Rev. Martin spoke up: "With all due respect, Governor, I'm not a boy. That's the trouble with this part of the country. They don't recognize the manhood of the Negro. But they will some day."

The delegation spokesman explained the business of the visit. Their main purpose was to secure permission to have a private physician make a thorough examination of Herndon.

The governor referred to the State Prison Commissioner's statement and said there was no need for outside aid. "If outsiders would stop meddling in Georgia's affairs, there would be no trouble. The law would take its course. Georgians resent Northern interference."

"We're quite willing that the private physician should be a resident of Georgia. But he must be competent and unbiased."

"I know what you're getting at," Talmadge said, speaking in very moderate tones. "You're hinting at mistreatment of the negra in Georgia. Well, that's a lie."

Then, addressing me, he said, "Ben, your father gets along all right here. He's given you a better education than even most white boys get. Isn't that so?"

"As long as any Negro refrains from challenging this damnable lynch system, he'll get along somehow."

The governor, still mild: "Ben, you've been sent up nawth to school. I know all about it. You got too much education to love your own state. . . . What about you, Reverend? You seem to be doing all right?"

"Governor, I've been wanting to say this to you for a long time. I'm now living in Atlanta because I escaped being lynched in my little Georgia home town several years ago. Negroes are not treated like human beings in this state, and the whole world knows it. I'm one of the few hundred who vote in this state. In 1932, I voted the Communist ticket, not because I know much about communism but because I'll vote for any party that offers me and my people a square deal. I'm going to continue to vote that way until I get my rights. I'm a minister of the gospel. I believe in equality and brotherhood. I vote and act the way I preach."

This just about put the finishing touches to the interview. The governor rose: "Well, I'll make a further investigation of the situation and let you hear from me. Leave your names and addresses. Sorry, I have another appointment."

The governor had failed in his effort to separate the Negroes from the whites. He had tried to intimidate Rev. Martin and me, trading on the fact that we would be living in the state after the delegation had gone. That failed. He tried to insult the delegation with snide references to Northern "outsiders." That didn't work. Then, bursting with suppressed indignation, he fled the scene.

He did report on his "later investigation," asserting that to charge that the State of Georgia was mistreating its prisoners was an insult to the people of Georgia. At about this time, Robert E. Burns' book *I'm a Fugitive from a Georgia Chain-Gang*, was shocking the nation. As a result of the pressure of public opinion, the state of New Jersey refused to honor Georgia's warrant for the extradition of Burns, an escaped Georgia convict. The mistreatment of Herndon—carried out secretly because of the widespread publicity in the case—was minor beside the torture and killings that inmates suffered in the Georgia penal system.

I had become wholly immersed in the mass campaign. But soon the appeal had to be made to the Georgia State Supreme Court. As much as I hated to tear myself from the vital campaign to expose the horrors of the Georgia penal system, I had to give first attention to the appeal. I suffered from one major handicap that went back to my days in law school. Practical court work and brief-making were not part of the school's official curriculum. These practical, indeed indispensable, subjects were taken up through law clubs run by students under faculty supervision. Actual cases were contrived and distributed among the clubs and argued before mock tribunals. It was a vital part of the students' education—and one that I had missed entirely, because I had protested being assigned to an all-Negro club. Protests to the board were unavailing, and when I waited on Dean Roscoe Pound, he ignored my statement that Negro first-year students were being segregated—in violation of the policies of the university—and said, "The law clubs are a very important part of preparation for the law. I'd advise that you enter one and stay in it until you finish the course."

"I'm sorry, sir, but I'll never enter a segregated law club voluntarily. I'll just miss it."

"That's up to you," he said, almost absentmindedly, "you'll miss it later."

This incident stood out in my mind throughout my three years at Harvard and for a long time afterwards. Here was a ranking law school, considered in some circles as the country's finest, teaching the impartiality and equality of the law, but which built segregation right into the process of teaching law.

The dean was right: I "missed the law club work" and it caught up with me as I prepared the brief for the appeal to the State Supreme Court. For about ten days I withdrew from all other activity except my law books and a mountain-high stack of paper. Geer and I completed the brief in about a week, but I felt that the case was too important to be left wholly in our inexperienced hands. I called the ILD national office and asked them for the assistance of an experienced practitioner in constitutional and civil rights cases to give our brief the once-over.

It was at this point that I was introduced to a woman of brilliant mind and pure heart—Carol King. Her help was invaluable; the brief which we submitted in Georgia Supreme Court was virtually her entire handiwork. It contained all the points I had, with so much travail, assembled, but they were put into presentable and legally forceful shape. More important, the brief contained telling arguments I would not have thought of in a million years. It commanded the respect of the six-judge Georgia tribunal; indeed, after the decision was arrived at, one of the justices called me to commend it.

Carol King was a remarkable personality—generous, warm, dynamic, self-sacrificing—yet objective. She was frank and jovial, brushing away attitudes of male supremacy with contempt. She was indefatigable, even though a chronic back ailment found her in frequent pain. Her mind was quick and penetrating in all phases of the law, particularly constitutional law. (She subsequently became known for her expertness in immigration law and in civil rights.) She could have had a fabulously lucrative career, but she devoted her life to principles, to the victims of class justice. When she died, in 1952. I felt I had lost a close relative; we had worked so often together—an experience which forms the strongest type of bond between people. . . .

I became a member of the bar of the Georgia Supreme Court barely in time—in fact, the day before the Herndon appeal was placed on the docket for argument. It was my first time before

this court, but I felt none of the nervousness that had characterized my first moments in the trial session. I made a spirited, even
brash, presentation of the appeal. I spoke for about 50 minutes,
developing the constitutional question of free speech. I lectured
the court as if they were undeveloped and confused students.
They watched me in utter contempt and asked no questions.
The state attorney spoke afterward; and no one asked him a
single question. I was offered time for rebuttal, but I declined,
saying, "The state has offered nothing worthy of the court's
serious attention. I waive rebuttal."

In entering the appeal, the state had cut the guts out of the
transcript, expunging the very substance of the prejudiced conduct of the trial. I called these shocking omissions to the attention of the court. But my protests fell on deaf ears. I scrambled
around for several days trying to remedy this monstrous situation
—but finally I had to accept the crooked record or lose my chance
to appeal.

Although the word "nigger" was expunged, the word "darkey"
to which I had taken strong objection was retained. But when
the State Supreme Court handed down its decision, it held that
there was no opprobrium or prejudice attached to the use of
that term as applied to Negroes in a court of law.

The opinion of the court was extensive, even labored. When
it was handed down, I received an unexpected call to come to
the office of the State Supreme Court. I went into a private office
to confront none other than Chief Justice Richard B. Russell,
father of Senator Russell. Talking in a somewhat condescending,
patronizing tone, he said he had not participated in the decision.
He merely wanted to give me "a few words of advice."

"Never refer contemptuously to the arguments of the state's
attorneys," he admonished. "And try not to become involved in
such cases." When I tried to discuss this with him, he said he
did not wish to discuss the matter. He only wanted to set me
straight at the beginning of my career. It was just another instance of the "gentle pressure" that had been gratuitously applied
since I had been in the case.

The next step was the appeal to the U.S. Supreme Court. I

passionately wanted to participate in these legal proceedings, but it was out of the question because I did not have the necessary legal stature or experience—and I knew it. And I was far more interested in making sure that Herndon got the best legal talent available. Besides all this, I was not eligible to practice before the U.S. Supreme Court. One has to be a member of the bar of the highest court of resort in a state for three years before being eligible for U.S. Supreme Court practice, and I had less than one year when the appeal was processed in Washington.

I conferred with the ILD national office in securing proper counsel. The attorneys obtained were men of prestige, experience and ability—Whitney North Seymour,* former U.S. Solicitor-General, and Walter Gellhorn, a Columbia University law professor. They were given a free hand in handling the appeal.

The Herndon case was finally won in the U.S. Supreme Court by five to four. The case had gone before the tribunal twice. The first time the majority held that the constitutional question was not properly put before the court. Justices Cardozo, Brandeis and Holmes, however, had filed vigorous dissents, so I felt I was in good company. Shortly after this first negative decision, counsel for Herndon decided upon a blank attack on the conviction. Herndon, then free on bail, was voluntarily surrendered to the Georgia state authorities. After he was taken into custody, a writ of habeas corpus was filed, attacking the constitutionality of the Georgia insurrection law. The mass movement around the defense got its second wind.

And, lo and behold! the Georgia District Court—Judge Hugh M. Dorsey—declared the law unconstitutional. His favorable decision was one of those situations that confound the ruling class

---

* Later, in 1952 at the height of the McCarthy-McCarran witch-hunt, Seymour in a speech before the American Bar Association urged the disbarment of any lawyer who serves as counsel for a Communist. He was evidently trying to clear his own skirts for having contended in the U.S. Supreme Court, 16 years before, that a lowly Negro American Communist was guaranteed the right to his own political views and that any state law proscribing this right was a violation of the U.S. Constitution.

—coming as it did from one of its own circle. Dorsey was a maverick who frequently displayed independence from the political machine. When he made the Herndon decision, the white supremacists fell on him like wolves devouring a sheep. And the state appealed, carrying the case once more to the U.S. Supreme Court. The court majority could not turn down the appeal, since, by its own previous negative decision, it had unwittingly left the door open. Since the constitutional question had not been before it in the previous appeal, it had never been adjudicated. The habeas corpus placed the constitutional question squarely before the court for the first time.

Final victory came in 1937, five years after Herndon's arrest and four years after his trial. It was a triumph for free speech, free press, free assembly—hailed everywhere by the democratic people of the country. It also had repercussions on the Negro issue, around which it had been fought. Shortly after the decision, Georgia placed its first Negroes on jury panels.

Occasionally, during the Herndon case, I had handled some relatively small cases. One case brought me perilously close to disbarment. Prior to Herndon's arrest, the case of the "Atlanta Six" involved the Georgia insurrection law. The "Atlanta Six"— two white women, two white men and two Negro men—had made street-meeting speeches in 1930 on the question of mass unemployment. They were arrested, indicted and then granted bail. They were never brought to trial; after the Herndon case their indictments were quashed. As to why they were never brought to trial I can only speculate that the Georgia politicians were afraid of the Negro-white unity that might have been touched off by a trial. A conviction was easier in the case of a lone Negro, than where white defendants were involved.

While the Herndon case was passing through the Georgia courts, the ILD retained me to negotiate a transfer of bondsmen for the Atlanta Six. The two white women returned to Atlanta, and I became their attorney, having secured two Negro businessmen to substitute as their bondsmen. When we appeared in court, the result was a circus. As I spoke, representing the white women, you could hear a mouse walking on cotton. The judge, thrown into utter confusion by this "daring challenge" to hallowed practice, sought to ignore me altogether and talk to the women. But they referred him constantly to me.

A few days later I received a call from an attorney—a friend of my father's—advising me that disbarment proceeding against me were under consideration. He explained that the real reason was my acting as attorney for white women, but that the overt reason was to be my violation of the jim-crow laws of the city and state. But discretion proved the better part of valor, better even than white supremacy sometimes. Probably the powers that be feared the unfavorable publicity that would result from such proceedings, and its effect on the Herndon case. What the State of Georgia feared to attempt, the "angelic" Judge Medina did sixteen years later when he moved to disbar attorneys in the Smith Act case against eleven Communist leaders in Foley Square.

After the Herndon case—indeed, after the trial—the whole situation changed for me. Where formerly I had received the relatively benign cooperation and tolerance of the city's ruling circles, I now was, at best, regarded with suspicion and, at worst, as a rooshan-inspired Bolshevik.

A couple of weeks after the trial, I came to my office in the Odd Fellows building. My desk was located directly opposite a wooden paneled door in the facing wall. My desk chair faced the door, which opened out into another office. I sat down at my desk and suddenly I noticed a metal tube sticking through a hole bored into the door and pointing directly at me. I got up and examined it. I found a piece of paper stuck into the tube. I took it out and read: "The Ku Klux Klan rides again. Georgia is no place for bad niggers and red Communists. Next time we'll shoot. (signed) The Ku Klux Klan."

It was a metal tube all right—the barrel of a revolver.

Geer and I got the landlord and had the paneled door opened. We took the revolver and turned it over to the police. That was the last we heard of it; not a word appeared in the papers about

it; the police probably turned it over to its Ku Klux owner—
with apologies.

I told my father about it. He was shocked to learn that nothing
had been done by the police, so he himself took it up with the
police authorities—thus revealing that he was more naive than
his "whippersnapper" son. He came back even more shocked and
a trifle beaten in spirit.

"They knew all about it, son. But they say there's nothing they
can do, unless something happens." (Which meant, I suppose,
after I had been lynched.) "But then, son, they tried to get me
to get you out of this case. I told them you were a lawyer and
entitled to defend any client whom you represented. In other
words, they tried to put pressure on me to make you desert your
client because he's a Communist. I would never do such a thing,
son. I can't see that you're getting anywhere going too far into
this communism. But I wouldn't think much of you as a lawyer
or my son if you deserted your client."

"That I'll never do, dad. Once you challenge their system,
the fundamental oppression of Negroes, you are put beyond the
pale of the law. You have quite a standing among the leaders
of this city, but you see it doesn't amount to much where your
son is involved. The Klan and the police are virtually the same."

What had become clear to the class-conscious Georgia officials
had also become clear to large sections of the Negroes on the
street. The defense policies we had pursued in the Herndon case
gave them a lift; they were glad to see the lily-white system challenged. They had too long smarted under the insulting practice
of addressing Negroes as "niggers" in the Georgia courts. In their
own ways they found methods of communicating their solidarity
to me, of lending encouragement, moral support. Perhaps they
gave me too much credit because they saw me as a tribune trying
to right long-endured injustices. In a sense, they cast me in this
role, and I deeply appreciated their confidence.

As the instrument of this challenge I made many mistakes—
many political, some legal. But I do not think that they were of
such a major character as to jeopardize the outcome. Indeed, the
social issues in the case were so historic, so universal that they

Benjamin J. Davis, 1946

Ben Davis in the 1930's

Ben Davis as a young man, with his father and mother

Paul Robeson congratulating Ben Davis on his
election to the City Council in 1943

The councilman's Harlem office

Addressing a Soviet Friendship rally in Carnegie Hall, 1946

On a picket line in Harlem

*Posters in Harlem during the
amnesty campaign*

A mass rally at 126th. St. and Lenox Ave. in Harlem greeted Ben Davis
on his release from House of Detention on bail pending appeal against
Smith Act verdict. Paul Robeson is at the microphone, and Ben Davis
is receiving flowers.

Inspecting a Harlem tenement

Campaigning for State Senator on the Peoples Party ticket, 1964

Peter V. Cacchione

With Eugene Dennis and William Z. Foster (center), then General
Secretary and Chairman, respectively, of Communist Party, 1947

*At City College, New York City, during a free speech fight
after his release from prison*

eventually overcame the errors I had made in the defense. For these issues set into motion millions of workers and democratic-minded people whose raised voices finally secured the freedom of Angelo Herndon and helped to plant the seeds of freedom and equality which will one day break through the thistles of white supremacy and capitalist exploitation.

The Herndon case was my first lesson in mass defense, as distinct from the reformist methods used by the NAACP, whose leaders saw the legal defense as the be-all and end-all of every struggle. There had been two alternative lines of policy open in the Herndon case. The reformist policy would have "defended" Herndon as an isolated individual victimized by the excesses of an otherwise sound capitalist order, thus objectively sustaining the lynch system of national oppression. This approach could have had important variations—from the crude Uncle Tomism of throwing the defendant on the mercy of the court to a militant attack upon significant but secondary factors, such as the discriminatory conduct of the trial. Implicit in the latter is the view that the trial in itself was justified, but should be conducted fairly. It would deny the class and social roots of the trial. As a result, the defendant would have been put on trial instead of the social system under which the trial was taking place. Once the social roots of the case were denied or overlooked, mass participation in the defense of Herndon was also likely to be ignored.

Thus, under the reformist approach, the fate of the defendant is determined primarily by the legalistic skill of the defense counsel—against the concerted legal skill of the prosecution, backed up by all the pressures at the command of the ruling class which controls the judicial system. The class struggle—the essence of the judicial struggle—is thus concealed, or at least blunted.

It cannot be denied that legal victories are often won by this reformist method; and often they have favorable social implications. But more often such victories are partial, hollow or ephemeral.

Pressures of a reformist nature were put upon our law firm in the Herndon case, though disguised in many ways. The open lynch pressures, of course, were always present; and my rights as defense counsel were crudely and brutally denied in the course of the trial. But there were also attempts to win me over by "tender persuasion" or to buy me out, in which efforts were made to use even my father as a tool. Late in 1932, the Republican Party offered me a highly lucrative post on a campaign tour in the East and Midwest on behalf of Herbert Hoover's presidential ticket—"like father, like son," was the implication. I was to be beaten with the club or politically seduced with carrots—whichever way would bring me over. The Southern Committee on Inter-racial Cooperation in Atlanta tried hard gently to persuade me that although there was merit to my case, my "methods were wrong"—I was causing too much "publicity and ill-feeling"; I should work more "quietly," like Channing Tobias perhaps.

The really new thing about the Herndon case was not my role as defense counsel. It was the break with the reformist policy and the promulgation of a working class defense policy in the deep South. The essence of that policy was to present the Herndon case as an out-and-out frame-up that should never have been brought to trial; the indictment itself contravened the basic right of free speech and free assembly guaranteed by the Bill of Rights. Our policy saw the Herndon case as an extension of the class struggle into the judicial arena and it sought to unmask the brutal nature of that struggle in all its dimensions. The real criminals that should be put in the dock were the administrators, benefactors and rulers of the white supremacy system. We sought to make clear that the victims of that system were the poor whites as well as the poor blacks who were held in submissive division while the ruling class exploited and oppressed both, imposing upon the Negro an extra burden of racist persecution.

Since Herndon was the victim of the Southern ruling class, only the working class and the Negro people could save him by their mass counter-pressure, exerted unitedly and by every militant democratic means. Defense counsel thus acted as the tribune of the oppressed class and was most effective when he expressed, in legal and constitutional terms, the policies of the working class. In this way, he gave his client the strongest and best defense. At the same time, he struck hard and directly at the whole capitalist system of national oppression of the Negro people, seeking to free not only this Angelo Herndon but thousands of others still to come. It was an injunction to the masses that if you want to save Angelo Herndon and others like him you must defeat, change and eventually replace capitalism with a better system, socialism.

It was by no means a quirk of the Communists not to put all their eggs in the court basket. The experiences of the past half century show that to put one's trust in the high judiciary to uphold the constitutional rights of Negroes is like leaving the cat to watch the milk. The entire complicated and official structure of segregation and discrimination rests upon precedents and decisions of that court. Every now and then the U.S. Supreme Court will modify these precedents, or make concessions when compelled by public opinion, but it is still to declare illegal the whole body of anti-Negro laws and practices which nullify the federal constitution. The concessions it grants are to make the underlying system of national oppression of the Negro more invulnerable, less susceptible to attack. For example, the highly praised decision of the Supreme Court in the "restrictive covenant" cases was but a pyrrhic victory. It held that "restrictive covenants" could not be enforced by the courts—but, in reality, these laws are not enforced by the courts as such, but by mob violence and lynch terror. Not one Negro ghetto has been broken down by the Supreme Court decision. The real estate interests who make super-profits out of these ghettos are too large and influential for the high court to dry up their source.

As an ideology, reformism seeks gains in order to strengthen capitalism, to abate the class struggle, and to prevent accession to state power of the working class. Thus it comes to pass that Negro leaders, militant in earlier periods in the movement for progressive reforms, do at times become instruments of capitalists when they seek to block the emergence of the Negro working class and its allies as the new—and necessary—leaders of the Negro people in their effort to achieve full national liberation. Others among them—stalwart in their integrity and understanding—break with reformism as an ideology and become partisans of the working class, realizing that under conditions of modern monopoly capitalism this class can achieve the equality and freedom of the Negro people.

Communists are not opposed to reforms. On the contrary, they work constantly for the slightest improvements that can be won within the framework of capitalism. They are willing to unite and cooperate with all forces for the betterment of the people's conditions, in any and all fields of endeavor. At the same time, Communists believe that the struggle for reform should be carried on in such a way as to weaken and expose capitalism and to build up the forces that can bring about the replacement of capitalism by socialism. Communists are aware that reform victories tend to strengthen mass illusions about monopoly capitalism and therefore seek always to carry the struggle further and always to keep before the mass movement the socialist perspective.

The five-year sentence that I am now serving in Terre Haute federal prison only confirms many times over the correctness of my Communist convictions—first attained during the Herndon case—and only proves the cynical brutality of the ruling class and government toward the Negro people and toward those of their spokesmen who really fight for Negro liberation, who really challenge the fundamental economic and political causes of Negro oppression, and who seek to replace the barbarism of white supremacy with the noble virtues of human equality.

CHAPTER SIX

THE "IMPOSSIBLE" CANDIDATE

When, in 1943, my candidacy for the New York City Council on the Communist ticket was announced, the press was unanimous in declaring my election impossible. For entirely different reasons, some of my friends joined them. The difficulties were considered insurmountable.

Shortly after I was designated as a candidate by the Manhattan County Committee of the Communist Party, I telephoned my father in Atlanta to inform him of my nomination. I had run for office before on the Communist ticket; consequently my father was not inclined to attach any special importance to this particular instance. But I assured him that this was different—this time I was going to win. An old hand in politics, too worldly-wise to be moved by youthful enthusiasm, he replied:

"Son, this election is going to be like all the rest. Remember the time you ran for District Attorney or something on the Communist ticket? Well, you didn't get elected then; and you won't be elected this time. You Communists are always running for offices, but you never catch them. The day of your party hasn't come yet."

But the impossible happened. I was elected. The opposition and its two-party machine were shocked and dismayed. They had already had to swallow the bitter pill of the election of Peter V. Cacchione, Brooklyn Communist leader, in 1941, and they had hoped to get rid of him in 1943. Instead, they were now faced with two Communists in the city council.

My friends and supporters were jubilant. My election was another high-water mark in the achievement of the labor-Negro people's progressive coalition. Independent political action had scored a signal victory. And the Negro people of Harlem, demonstrating tremendous political maturity, had fired a shot that was heard not only in the sharecropper's cabin in Mississippi, but in the trenches in Europe and the Far East. It was, above all, a victory for unity behind our country's patriotic, national war to defeat the Rome-Berlin-Tokyo axis.

The combination of circumstances and relationships which had led to this triumph had thrust upon me the honor of being the first Negro Communist elected to office in the history of the United States. While I regarded it as a great distinction and an unprecedented opportunity, uppermost in my mind was the feeling of responsibility. My task was not only to advance the movement which alone could improve the jim-crow conditions imposed upon my community in Harlem, but also to make the whole of New York City a better place for the people. There was no contradiction, but rather a dynamic unity, between the two.

A part of the campaign against me was that I would never get elected because I had two strikes against me. I was a Negro and a Communist. An amusing incident as to this "deadly" combination occurred when I called my father the night I was elected. He thought it was a gag and wouldn't believe me. I finally gave up—I knew how stubborn father could be, especially when he had predicted another outcome.

The next morning I got a call from him. Excited and happy, he exclaimed: "Son, I guess you were right. I see there's a headline in the paper here which says 'Black Red elected in New York. White Yankees vote for him.' "

My father represented a link between the period of the struggle for Negro rights in which he had lived and fought and another stage of this struggle in which I was living and fighting. He still was inclined to think his period would last forever, and still believed pretty much, as did Frederick Douglass, that "the Republican Party was the ship, and all else was the sea." He found it difficult to acknowledge the beginning of another era. Before he died, however, he had become somewhat reconciled to the inevitable; he even went so far as to completely forgive my abandonment 28 years earlier of the comfortable and lucrative bourgeois career he had arranged for me.

The reaction of the Atlanta paper was a small measure of the shock sustained by the bourgeoisie. The New York *Herald Tribune* sought to explain my election on the basis of my "personal following." Other papers and bourgeois experts on elections said it was a political accident.

Often in my campaign I would share with the audience the episodes involving my father. They never failed to get a big laugh, especially when there were many Southern-born Negroes among the listeners. For they were intimately acquainted with the utterly absurd—as well as murderous—forms that white supremacy could take in the deep South. Sometimes I would use the description of me as a "Black Red" to answer the favorite argument of A. Philip Randolph, the Social-Democratic Negro labor leader: "Why should the Negro add to the handicap of being Black, the handicap of being Red?"

Far from considering it a handicap to be a Negro and a Communist simultaneously, I considered it a double weapon against the ruling class. An American Negro has a background of 300 years of oppression in this country, and great indeed is the Negro's anger. When that same Negro is a Communist, he is equipped with a science—Marxism-Leninism—which alone can help realize his 300-year aspiration for freedom and equality.

In 1943, the only Negro member of the city council was Adam Clayton Powell, Jr., who had been elected as the first Negro member in 1941. He had been elected pretty much as an independent, securing designations from the City Fusion Party, the American Labor Party and the Democratic Party. He was the symbol of the progressive people's coalition in the city. This was the dramatic start of Powell's political power as an independent, when he first proclaimed his motto: "I will wear no man's collar." He was swept into office in 1941 on the crest of a wave of demands by the Negro people and their supporters for representation in the city legislature. His election was made possible technically by Proportional Representation, which had become the law of the city under the new Charter adopted in 1936.

Powell was a powerful orator, dramatic and colorful, and capable of manipulating the emotions of his audience. A shrewd politician, he had the gift of sensing the popular yearnings and trends of the masses, which he voiced as their leader. His church, the Abyssinian Baptist, built by his father, was famous as the largest in the United States, numbering 15,000 members. A wealthy institution, its members were very politically and nationally alert, and constituted a formidable election machine.

As the chief executive functionary of the Harlem Communist Party, I had a deep concern in having the community retain the seat held in trust, as it were, by Councilman Powell. I had heard that he did not intend to run for re-election but, putting no stock in rumors, I decided to have a personal talk with him. We had a long discussion, a friendly one, but not successful, on the question of the city council. He said, in effect, that he had already announced his candidacy for congress in 1942. The new congressional district which made it possible to elect a Negro representative from Harlem had been carved out in 1941, and Powell was determined to be the first Negro congressman from that district.

I placed the issues squarely before him, giving the point of view of my party, namely, that it was incumbent upon the progressive forces of the community to do everything possible to guarantee the retention by a Negro of the seat he now held and, if at all possible, to elect an additional Negro. I emphasized that we were faced with the prospect of losing the one place in the council, and that would amount to a setback of such proportions as to damage the united struggles of the Negro people. I asked him to reconsider his decision not to run and, failing that, to assist in establishing unity around a progressive Negro candidate of independence and integrity who would be worthy of support.

Powell declined on both scores. He stated that to run for re-election to the city council in 1943 and then to make the race for congress in 1944 was more than he could bear either physically or financially, and that he considered it best to relinquish his position in the council in order to prepare for the congressional race in 1944. On the second point, he preferred a hands-off policy.

This was late spring of 1943 and time was passing rapidly. It

would be no easy or simple matter to achieve Harlem unity
around a candidate who could win and there was not much time
left. I had heard that Dr. Channing Tobias was considering the
race and made an appointment with him at his offices in the
YMCA headquarters on Madison Avenue. He was, of course,
neither as militant nor as close to the man on the street as
Powell, although he was pro-labor and had associated himself
on various occasions with the progressive coalition. He would
have made a good candidate at that time; he was part of the
Roosevelt coalition among the Negro people in a vague sort of
way. He was a typical liberal, but I was not looking for a Communist candidate but one around whom the broadest unity of
the Negro people and labor could be achieved in this specific
situation.

When I placed the question before him, he respectfully declined, on the ground that he wanted to remain independent
politically and had no desire for public office.

I finally went to Dr. George Cannon, who later became the
chairman of the non-partisan committee for my election. Although he declined to run, he helped in every way, calling conferences, having personal chats with friends, trying to convince
representative Negroes to run.

George Cannon was an able physician and surgeon who had
not lost any of his youthful passion against jim-crow. He would
not sacrifice his militant views to further his medical career, and
although he was a Roosevelt Democrat, he did not quail at my
Communist convictions, but rather believed that if a cause was
worthy, people should not permit political or other differences
to prevent them from supporting it.

Nevertheless, the problem had not been solved. The nomina-
tions for the city council by all parties had been made, but no
representative Negro from Harlem had been nominated. The
Democrats had not nominated a Negro. Even the Negro Tammany leaders in the community were up in arms. They felt they
had been put in a very bad position before the Negro people,
upon whom they depended in the election district for the Dem-

ocratic vote. Many of them protested and showed their disapproval but without going so far as breaking with the Tammany machine.

Our Harlem Communist Party surveyed the situation, consulted with Negro and labor leaders. My own conversations with various Negro spokesmen demonstrated that all felt that the place in the council must not be lost. They felt that the failure of the two major parties to designate a candidate of the community's choice should be exposed during the campaign. Our party had nominated a candidate, Carl Brodsky, well known in labor and progressive circles. He offered to withdraw in my favor and to permit the party to substitute my name for his as candidate on the Communist ticket. After due consideration, the county committee made the switch and my name was substituted for Brodsky's within the time permitted by the law. This decision was based upon the record of our Harlem party among the Negro people, their response to its program, and on the basis of our contact with the community. At least, I was an integral part of the people's coalition in Harlem, had shared in their struggles and activities, and had been accepted as one of their recognized spokesmen. Moreover, as my election proved, our party had correctly judged the desires and sentiment of the Negro people and their white supporters as well.

The honor of my designation as the Communist candidate belonged rightfully not to me but to the people from whom I sprang. Whatever spark of determination I possessed in the struggle was instilled in me by the hardihood of my people in resisting oppression in America, Africa, the West Indies and wherever black men fight to live. I had seen that same flame burn in my father; a little of it burns in every Negro, if he does not permit it to be extinguished by violence or intimidation, or if he does not deny it for a mess of pottage.

Carl Brodsky was truly a representative of the Jewish people. In withdrawing in my favor, under circumstances in which the Jewish people needed a representative in the City Council, he demonstrated the close bonds of cooperation that could exist between the Jewish and Negro people. His action was a warm, human and generous symbol of recognition on the part of progressive Jewish workers of their own profound stake in the cause of Negro liberation.

It was not only I who was deeply impressed; this dramatic and genuine demonstration of solidarity was not lost among the people of Harlem. Although Brodsky spent most of his time during the campaign trying to win the lower East Side Jewish workers to my support, he would occasionally come to Harlem, often speaking on the same platform with me. He would receive a rousing ovation from the people.

The tremendous vote I received from the Jewish community was one of the highlights of my election. I was told by experienced election campaigners that my name had become as familiar as one of their own, and that never before had a Negro candidate received such a high percentage of votes in a white neighborhood.

The metropolitan newspapers merely noted the fact that I had been substituted for Carl Brodsky. I was listed along with the candidates of the other parties. After this, there ensued a conspiracy of silence in these papers; the bourgeois election experts and commentators paid me no mind. I didn't have a chance, according to them, so why waste printer's ink? Tammany paid no serious attention to my candidacy; nor did the Republicans. This attitude even affected the people in my own ranks. Many friends said, "Yes, you'll make a good campaign, a very fine one indeed; but you won't be elected—too many odds against you. Besides, the two party machines are too strong; if you look as though you might become a serious threat, they'll pour in thousands of dollars to defeat you," and so on, ad infinitum.

These friends and supports were not the only ones with serious doubts. Some of my own comrades were skeptical. They were only a small minority among the party membership, still their views deserved serious consideration. They doubted that the estimate of a possible victory was correct, although during the campaign they worked with great skill and energy; I would have liked to have had more "skeptics" like them. Such differences illustrate a cardinal distinction of our party—a working class organization operating on the principle of democratic centralism.

Once a decision was made it was binding and carried out by all members alike. Some of these skeptics pointed out that a Communist councilmanic candidate in Manhattan had never received more than 13,000 votes, and in Harlem no more than 5,000 votes. They estimated that I would have to receive almost twice the number of votes in the trade union and progressive white areas that a Communist candidate had ever received in the whole of Manhattan under the best circumstances. Furthermore, the campaign was late and I had only a bare six weeks. Other arguments were that any attempt to shoot for victory would tax our organization too heavily and run the danger of not securing the re-election of Councilman Cacchione in Brooklyn. Still others held that I should aim to secure enough second-choice votes to elect the ALP candidate, which would be a big advance since Manhattan had never had a labor councilman.

These arguments could not be brushed aside willy-nilly. They proved to be very valuable in pitching and focusing the campaign and in touching up weak points. Besides, these exchanges of opinion were part of the thorough way in which our party considered all angles of a problem and then charted its course. It was this same Marxist consideration of many-sided factors that led to the election victory and rallied and strengthened our ranks.

All the doubts expressed by the skeptics failed to dent my enthusiasm. My campaign staff and I prepared to involve all these friends, not in a "very fine" campaign, but in a winning one. I was buoyed up by the fact of Pete Cacchione's election in 1941. What was basically new in the situation was the tremendous upsurge among the Negro masses and the unprecedented support they were receiving from white workers—particularly from the CIO, but also from the AFL—as well as from white intellectuals, artists, progressives, liberals. The Negro people, wholeheartedly supporting the war against fascist-racism abroad, were demanding more and more earnest of eventual victory at home. Their democratic aspirations were released under the impetus of the anti-fascist war. The war, under Roosevelt's leadership, brought forward the most democratic and progressive traditions of our country. What was apparent here was the possibility of a qualitative leap forward for the Negro people and for independent political action. It had to be grasped then or it would be lost.

The circumstances that had dictated my nomination also shaped my campaign, which was pitched upon the theme of winning the war and demonstrating against Hitler racism by advancing the cause of Negro representation at home. In the local and city program were: the banning of jim-crow in Stuyvesant Town, the appointment of a Negro on the Board of Education, a public market for Harlem, the end of police brutality, rent and price controls, slum clearance, the enforcement and expansion of the multiple dwelling laws, and the outlawing of all forms of racial discrimination, anti-Semitism, jim-crow and segregation.

But I was also running on the Communist ticket. It was my duty and responsibility, as well as my privilege, to explain to the voters why I was running on that ticket, what the Communist Party stood for and why I was a member. If I couldn't trust the people, why should they trust me? I did not believe in hiding "the light of Marxism-Leninism" under a bushel. It was necessary to point out that though I had backers of other parties in my corner, I nevertheless was a Communist whose program went much farther than the present election campaign; that I believe in socialism and would ever strive for its triumph at home.

My campaign spread like wildfire. Overnight the nonpartisan committee for my election leaped from about 50 to approximately 2,000—a real cross-section of ministers, doctors, lawyers, businessmen, trade unionists, social leaders, women, youth, foreign-born, native-born, workers, artists—indeed, people from every conceivable stratum of life. The committee became so large and unwieldy that it had to divide up into smaller committees. The major power in these committees and among the campaign workers were the Negro masses and the trade unionists. The accomplishments of our party, which numbered less than 2,000, were nothing short of miraculous. Only hard work, devotion and skill—climbing six and seven flights of stairs, tramping the streets in the roughest weather, seeing ministers, arranging conferences, holding street meetings, distributing literature, and so on—could achieve such "miracles."

Resolutions of endorsement and support soon began to pour

in from unions, churches, groups of almost every description. Friends in the deep South, especially from Atlanta, sent long public statements of good wishes, accompanied by donations. Soldiers in the trenches sent best wishes. The campaign took on an international aspect. The two Harlem Negro weeklies reflected in as much space as they dared to give the snowballing character of the campaign.

A group of artists and layout experts produced excellent campaign literature. An enterprising chap even got hold of an old Amherst yearbook of my class (1925)—from an unsuspecting Wall Street classmate—and reproduced my entire college career in pictures. My campaign literature was of "printer's excellence"; even experienced Democrats and Republicans wanted to know whether they could borrow my layout staff—"for a price," of course. They were amazed to find that not everyone was for sale. Many of the people of Harlem wanted certain campaign pieces as ornaments for their walls.

We held street rallies at the liveliest corners in Harlem, in the garment workers' district, before union and people's organizations in the course of their regular meetings. It was impressive to see the revolutionary tradition of the Negro church assert itself during the campaign. They became bulwarks of support to my campaign. Ministers invited me to speak "for a few minutes" at their 11 o'clock Sunday morning religious services.

The campaign was becoming irresistible; the smell of victory was in the air. Councilman Powell was now ready to take his stand. He issued a statement declaring that I was the "worthy successor" to his seat in the city council, and called upon his supporters and friends to vote for me. Accurately gauging the enthusiasm of the campaign, the Non-Partisan Committee decided on a rally in Golden Gate Ballroom—a mammoth auditorium in the center of Harlem, holding about 5,000 people.

A top price of $2.75 was placed on reserved seats and 50¢ on general admission. "Who ever heard of charging for admission to an election rally?" the doubting Thomases said. "Most candidates are only too glad to get a full house, with free admission." But the committee wouldn't be daunted.

There was scarcely a name band or a popular entertainer who did not volunteer their services. The Golden Gate was sold out ten days before the rally. On the day of the event, the fire department closed the hall two hours before the performance. When I appeared on the scene, it was all I could do to get in. One of the more prominent artists had to intercede with the police and fire department in my behalf.

Finally another 5,000 people had gathered outside the Golden Gate. We decided to rent an additional hall about six blocks away. We then routed the artists to this hall after their Golden Gate performance.

There were no speeches. Paul Robeson introduced me at both halls. I told the audience that I was but a part in a cause much bigger than any one of us and that we would struggle jointly until our country and the world were rid of Hitler racism and all humankind could live in dignity and walk in freedom.

This type of campaign rally was new, and we continued with it. At our street corner rallies we featured outstanding Negro and white artists. They performed with dignity, and they gave their talent because of their convictions.

In Harlem, support came from all sorts of quarters and for all sorts of reasons. A score or more old-timers who were Georgia-born supported me because they knew and admired my father. Some of them would slap me on the back and say: "Davis, your father was a Lincoln Republican. You must be a Lincoln Communist. I'm going to vote for you."

The large vote I received from the Porto Rican community was indispensable to my victory. During the campaign two things struck me with great force: First, that the Porto Rican community in lower Harlem, victimized by discrimination, had no representation whatever at any level of government*; second,

* The so-called racial pattern of the United States must appear quite bewildering to the Porto Rican people. In New York they are jim-crowed and treated like Negroes. But here in Terre Haute federal penitentiary they are integrated with the white inmates, while the Negro is segregated. It shows the utter insanity of racism and dis-crimination.

that I could not speak Spanish. I resolved to do something to help correct both these conditions.

In the course of the five-week whirlwind campaign, the Communist Party had built a smooth and powerful people's election machine that cut across all party lines. It was based on the crusading spirit of the advanced trade unionists—the leaders of the working class. They had ties with thousands of families, churches and people's organization in Harlem and throughout the city. When they moved in their full strength, the whole community moved. Naturally, our heaviest concentration was in Harlem, for without a large base vote in Harlem, it was not possible to win.

When election day came, the trade unionists took over all our poll-watching assignments—most outstanding were the organized seamen, the furriers (CIO) and the food workers (AFL). Church women prepared hot coffee and sandwiches at various assembly spots on election day. Many elderly Negroes voted for the first time in their lives. As a candidate, I had the right to visit the polls—and I did. Whenever I walked in, there were cheers and assurances of victory.

The heaviest voting in New York City is done in the last two hours—between 5 and 7 PM, the period when the workers are returning from their jobs. At about 4:30 PM the worst downpour of the season started. It lasted until about 8 PM, an hour beyond the closing of the polls. All we could do was hope. I continued to visit the polls even during the downpour and was surprised to see that the polling places were crowded. We took heart from this.

When the polls closed, our task had just begun. The count began next morning and was to last about eight days. These days seemed like years. To watch the count is a bewildering, nerve-wracking experience. One had to be on his toes against vote stealing, chicanery, every conceivable brand of trickery—as well as some honest errors. The Democrats and Republicans held all the official positions as counters, tellers, etc., and they did not want me to win. And it later appeared that they planned to count me out.

From the first day of the count, I was leading the field. Radio commentators blasted out that this was the upset of the election. Actually, they were counting those districts which included Harlem. But after the first two or three days, my vote began to level off as the count reached other parts of the city. I remained among the first three, however, and five were to be elected. It seemed that my election was assured. But then the stealing began in earnest. The votes for me began to disappear from my table, and the closest Tammany candidates began to congregate around my table, seeking to create an incident. We appealed to Mayor La Guardia, to the Honest Ballot Association, to every clean-government group. Statements were issued informing the public of the conspiracy to count me out.

On the fourth day Pete Cacchione, his own election in Brooklyn now assured, brought his entire staff over to the Manhattan court to assist me. Soon after he arrived, I discovered that some of my Harlem districts were missing and hadn't been counted. One of the ablest of our party election workers demanded a halt to the count, and demanded the right to search for the missing votes. He dug through the huge pile, district by district, and found not only the missing votes we knew of but also some unknown ones. In all, 1,500 votes has been stacked away, stolen right before our eyes. How perilous this was could be seen in the fact that I won by a little over 2,000 votes. It was a dramatic moment.

When, at the end of the long, gruelling count, my election was announced, every Negro in the Armory jumped up and yelled. They were to maintain their representation in the city council and white supremacy had taken a licking. The machine had been beaten. The wrath of an aroused electorate outweighed the fraud, deceit, corruption and vote-stealing of the party bosses. The unity of Negro and white had done the "impossible." History had been made.

Major party lines had been badly shattered. In the whole of Manhattan in 1943, there were not more than 6,000 Communists. My vote was more than 43,000. My election represented a qualitative leap forward for the Negro people, for the Negro-labor

alliance and for our party. It was the result of years of conscientious and consistent work of the party in Harlem in the
battles of the Negro people. And it went far beyond the state
lines of New York, reflecting the leading role that Harlem plays
in the political thinking of the Negro, nationally. From all over
the country came messages of congratulations, greetings, best
wishes. And I felt a sense of responsibility to the Negro people,
nationally, and to fighters for Negro and colonial liberation all
over the globe.

In this campaign for the City council, as well as in my subsequent campaigns in 1945 and 1947, the dominant note was its
people's character. By this I mean that my platform which was
based upon the major issues facing the electorate was shaped in
such a manner as to facilitate the coming together of the largest
sector of the people in defense and extension of their all-round
welfare. Republican and Democratic voters rallied to my support
no less than independents. It was the difference between a narrow
partisan campaign designed to reach primarily those who agreed
with my Marxist socialist views, and a people's nonpartisan
campaign designed to reach those who could unite on immediate
issues such as housing, equality, police violence and civil liberties,
irrespective of their party affiliation or long-range political perspective. The latter was especially adapted to Harlem, characterized by the all-people's character of the movement against the
jim-crow ghetto system.

However, there was no contradiction between my being a Communist candidate and at the same time a people's candidate. The
two supplemented each other. Moreover, only such an approach
could guarantee Negro representation on the city council. Besides, living Marxism is itself the broadest approach to the mass
of people, encompassing all who work by hand and brain. Since
my party was part of the people's movement in its electoral coalition form, I could pledge the support of the Communists to this
broad people's platform. Some of my well-meaning supporters
who were either Democrats or Republicans hoped I would stop
there and go no further, fearing that an espousal of my views

would frighten away voters. I rejected this view. Some agreed, others tried to reconcile themselves with my position; but none bolted. My campaigns were an excellent example of the united or people's front in which many forces work together on a common platform, even though they disagree on many other important questions.

At the same time, the foundation of my victorious campaign was the alliance of the Negro people and important sections of the labor movement. Upon this foundation was erected the structure of mass support among all sections of the population. The solid vote of Harlem was not enough to elect me; I needed the trade union and white progressive vote. That was shown clearly after the ALP candidate was counted out, when I received enough second-choice votes from him to assure my election by a comfortable margin.

It was significantly shown in the elections that among the Negro people there was a tremendous trend toward independent political action, toward breaking with the two-party system. They also showed great solidarity and a high degree of political maturity. Cacchione's vote was scattered widely over the Borough of Brooklyn, while my base vote was largely in a single community, which rebuffed solidly any red-baiting during the campaign.

Although our party received such a fine reception in Harlem it failed to become a mass party in that community. The basic requisites were present, except for one: the will to do so. As the leader of the party in Harlem, I was making one of the biggest mistakes in my political life. For I had become, no less than many other party leaders, deeply influenced by the revisionism of Browder, which led to the liquidation of the party as an independent working class force. Our party began to merge with the masses of militants and progressives, losing its own identity. True, the party had played a significant role by drawing together and leading the combination of forces that achieved my election and made possible continued Negro representation on the city council at a crucial moment when all other parties failed to meet the test. All the more pity that we failed to build a strong, mass party in Harlem.

Our campaign did make clear certain important characteristics of our party. My candidacy did not result from a careerist desire to run for office, as is generally the case with other parties. It was a response to the needs of the given situation—to guarantee that the Negro people should not lose their place on the city council. My nomination came only after the party had offered its full support to other candidates, none of whom were Communists but who merited the support of the Negro people and had a good chance of winning. In fact, it had not occurred to me that I might be the candidate.

The campaign also showed that only a progressive Negro candidate could serve as the symbol of unity. A conservative Negro spokesman identified with either of the major parties could not have united the Negro people. Such a candidate would have led to disunity, to certain defeat and to the loss of the council seat. The ruling class can unite only on a reactionary program, the working class only on a progressive one.

Thus, now the so-called unity of the CIO and AFL behind the pro-imperialist policies of the top labor leadership is a false facade. Badly confused and temporarily hogtied by the collaborationist policies of the officialdom, predominant sections of the labor movement are following the line of least resistance behind their treacherous leadership, although a significant section opposes these policies. On the other hand, a positive policy, clearly put before the rank and file and courageously fought for, together with further experiences in struggle, can eventually turn the tide. So much the better for America. Let us hope that this will happen in time—in time to avert the third world war and the catastrophe into which the ruling class, abetted by the top labor officialdom, is pushing the nation.

My electoral victory rested upon years of conscientious and consistent work of the Communist Party in Harlem in the struggles of the Negro people. Many gave their lives or served in prison, victims of police brutality, frame-ups or what have you. Progress seems slow and then, all at once, when conditions are ready, it takes a big leap forward. Communist open-air speakers were pelted with cabbages and tomatoes by Garveyites back in

1929, but a dozen years later even the neo-Garveyites joined in my campaign. It is always toward the qualitative leap forward that the Communist works, for it is only in this way that socialism can be established. There is no such thing as capitalism gradually growing into socialism. But the Communist also works, even at the risk of his life, to prevent a qualitative step backward. For this can mean only one thing—fascism, which in our country might well be worse than Hitlerism.

CHAPTER SEVEN

IN THE CITY COUNCIL

The die-hards had predicted dire consequences for the city of New York following upon my entry into the municipal government—even though I was only one of 25 members of the city council. There was, of course, Peter Cacchione, and now here was another who was not only red but black. It was too much for them.

When, however, I took office on January 4, 1944, the earth remained unshaken by hurricanes, earthquakes or other "acts of God" to mark my satanic accession to power. City Hall did not fall down. And there were only a few threats to refuse me my seat. These came in the form of the perennial and anonymous "taxpayers' suit." This paper tiger had been routed by the people two years earlier when Pete Cacchione took his seat. But, on the whole, they decided not to turn the spigot on as I took office this time.

Late in November, I was about to arrange the details of taking my oath of office—a simple pledge to uphold the Constitution of the United States and of the state of New York—when I received word from Mayor La Guardia to come to his office. I did not have the slightest idea what it was all about.

When I walked into his office at City Hall, he greeted me in his own inimitable way. "Hello, councilman-elect. Congratulations." He was smiling.

"Hello, Mr. Mayor. Why did you send for me?"

He went on in a jesting tone. "Well, you're only a councilman-elect. If you want to be a councilman, you'd better get sworn in."

I relaxed. "Oh," I said. "I'm arranging for that in the next few days."

"Just what I thought. You have only a few more days. I'm

going to swear you in right now and get it over with. After all, under the Charter, I'm the chief magistrate of the city."

Before I could take this in, he had buzzed his secretary, cussed a few times when the buzzer didn't work, gotten hold of a Bible and a blank form of a councilman's oath, and I was sworn in.

"Now you're a councilman," he said, "and even if the Democrats try to pull a fast one on the first day of the council, you'll be ready. Best of luck to you. We'll get together during the council sessions and have a talk."

The solicitude and initiative Mayor La Guardia had shown in getting me sworn in gave rise to a thought or two in my mind. But no more than that; it was fairly obvious, even to a neophyte, that La Guardia was a practical politician, and that he had acted in accordance with his political position. He was a Roosevelt independent or New Dealer and expressed it formally by registering with the American Labor Party. His interest in me was undoubtedly based on strengthening his minority position in the city council against the Tammany majority. After all, I had a vote: Perhaps the occasion would arise when it would be decisive. At all times, indeed, it would be preferable to have my good will. A second consideration was that I was the only Negro in the council. In a certain sense his relations with me would symbolize his relations with the large population of Negro Americans in Harlem. I do not say that these were the specific reasons that motivated La Guardia—there probably were others. But he did not swear me in for personal reasons—I did not know him; indeed, I had never met him. On the contrary, I had led many a delegation to see him at City Hall in protests against police brutality, relief discrimination, Stuyvesant Town discrimination, jim-crow—and on many other issues. I had denounced his actions on Stuyvesant Town, and our party had waged a relentless campaign against the shortcomings of his administration—not the least of which was his arrogant attitude toward the Transport Workers Union and the Public Workers Union. So there was absolutely no basis for any special personal regard for me. . . .

Prior to the first session in January, the minority of the council had a meeting for organizational purposes. It was a heterogeneous minority, since every council member who was not in the Tammany majority was automatically a member of the minority; it made no difference whether he was in agreement with the Tammany side of the chamber. Obviously the physical division of the chamber into majority and minority had little or no relation to political principles.

Alfred Phillips, who sat on the minority side, was even more of a straitlaced reactionary than anyone on the Tammany side. His favorite comment was: "This is the American way." He uttered these words as if they were a magic incantation. Once, on the council floor, I spoke of the way Pepsi-Cola signs were defacing the scenery of the city—particularly in Queens. Phillips clambered to his feet to announce that the Communist member of the council was attacking business. "These signs are the American way." And then he sat down as though he had uttered mankind's final and eternal wisdom. Pete and I nicknamed him "the American way," and privately we shuddered for America.

One of the most important things I learned at the preliminary minority session was that it was utterly impossible to whip that group into an organized, politically unified body, even on a minimum progressive program. How, for example, could Pete and I agree with the outlook of a man like "American way" Phillips? About the only things we agreed upon were: the election of a leader, the seating arrangement of the minority on the council floor, and the issuance of a statement setting forth in broad outline the policy we would pursue. Political expediency prevailed in all three actions. The statement carefully skirted the fundamental convictions of all of us.

Councilmen belonging to the same party sat together. Pete and I sat side by side from the first session of the council until the day he died. His near-blindness made this imperative anyway. I had known Pete and his record in the party and in the veterans' and unemployed movements for many years, but I had not worked with him personally. Our first day in the council was the beginning of a close association and of an enduring friendship. . . .

The first session of the council took place the first Wednesday after January 1, in accordance with the City Charter. It was purely a formal session and did not do any legislating. Pete had warned me not to be too impressed with the opposition—I had no difficulty whatsoever in not being impressed. Pete explained how the decisions, particularly those made by the Tammany majority, were not arrived at in debate on the floor but in the caucus rooms of Tammany Hall. I soon learned this for myself. For though the Tammany majority leader would go through the motions of defending a particular position, it was a mere formality. They had the votes and they played "power politics" in the council. Often some of us on the minority side would pick their arguments to pieces in debate, but it was like arguing with the Sphinx. Arguments, reason, common sense—no such "Communist propaganda" availed against Tammany. Only the superior power of great mass pressure could alter their position on any given issue.

The highlight of the first session was a brief address of welcome to new members by Newbold Morris. He made an innocuous liberal speech, of which I remember one portion: "The New York City Council is the most representative legislative body in the country, having among its members not alone Republicans and Democrats but saboteurs and Communists, women and men, Negro and white." This, he said, "was a demonstration of the kind of unity among the American people that was needed to win the war against Hitler." That impressed me because it was the nearest thing to an expression of the formal inclusion of Communists in national unity to win the war that I had ever heard from a white bourgeois politician—before or since.

The only other time I heard anything approaching such recognition was when the then Secretary of the Interior, the late Harold Ickes, campaigning for Roosevelt's fourth term, spoke in the Golden Gate Ballroom in Harlem to a packed audience of Negroes. He quoted liberally from a speech I had made attacking Dewey, mentioning me as author. Ickes, of course, did not intend to formalize recognition of the Communists. He was seeking a

broad channel into the Negro community in the interest of the
re-election of Roosevelt.*

Soon after my election I met with the leading committees of
our party in Harlem and on the state level, and with National
Committee members, to work out my responsibilities. The fundamental strength of such meetings was the collective thinking
of groups like these. Of course, the experience and advice of
Councilman Cacchione was of enormous value. Our party committee was only concerned with how I could best serve the people
of New York as a member of the city council. It was decided that
my main work was to be a councilman, which meant relinquish-
ing some of my party responsibilities; secondly, that my council
plan of work was to be divided into four parts—legislation, co-
ordinating my work in the council with the demands and needs
of the people, servicing the public and, finally, giving special
attention to the problems of the Negro people, the Harlem community, and labor. Councilman Cacchione and I were the links
between the parliamentary arena, on the one hand, and our
party and the working people, on the other.

On the floor of the council or in council committees, Pete and
I made our own decisions in what we believed to be the interests
of the working class and our Communist outlook. That's what
we were elected to do, and that's what we tried to do to the best
of our ability. A pertinent and amusing angle on the question of
our individual voting was that whenever one of the Tammany
hacks on the other side of the aisle was backed against the wall
in an argument, he would shout at the top of his voice that
Cacchione and I were voting on "orders from Moscow"; or, when
that seemed too farfetched, "on orders from 12th Street" (Communist headquarters). This they could do, mind you, without

* Seven years later, in 1951, Ickes wrote a column in the *New Republic*,
lumping together Paul Robeson and myself as "bright in school" and
"intelligent men," and wondering what caused us to become "agents of
a foreign power." Again, this red-baiting shows that expediency, not
principle, is the refuge of the bourgeois liberal in times of crisis. Moreover, he did the gifted Paul Robeson a grave disservice by lumping
him with me.

blinking an eye over the fact that they had just left Tammany headquarters, where corruption, graft and reaction called their tune.

Every week, Pete and I reviewed the legislation before the council and prepared whatever bills, resolutions or other measures we planned to introduce. We went over all the other bills, irrespective of their sponsors, analyzed their worth and acted on our convictions. Too much credit cannot be given to our secretarial assistants, to the legislative bureau of our party, to numerous trade unions and peoples' organizations, who gave us invaluable assistance. I owe a special debt of gratitude to the Negro people's organizations of Harlem and to many individual citizens, without whose counsel and aid I could not have functioned.

Altogether, during my first term, Pete and I introduced about 175 pieces of legislation. Only about 15 were passed, but nearly all of them had a salutary effect on the actions of the council. The substance of a bill was often taken from us and then passed as a Tammany measure. But Pete and I were happy to see it enacted, and considered our "pride of authorship" secondary. Neither Pete nor I ever denied that our legislation had propaganda purposes and content. I remember once saying on the council floor that a bill I had introduced for a municipal FEPC with teeth in it was not only a good bill, but it was good propaganda.

"Any propaganda that upholds the constitutional right of the Negro and minorities to equality of employment; any propaganda that upholds the 13th, 14th and 15th Amendments and the Declaration of Independence is good propaganda—to that kind of propaganda, I plead guilty," I said in debate.

Pete and I never failed to support any measure of any councilman which to any degree reflected the needs of the people of New York. The voters had crossed party lines in electing us, and we crossed party lines in upholding their best interests. But neither of us had illusions that we would break any records in obtaining the passage of legislation. We realized that the greatest value of our presence was that "we were tribunes of the labor-Negro-progressive movement."* On Pete's splendid initiative, he and I worked persistently to voice the demands of the people for local rent control legislation—a step which the Democrats, in obedience to the big realty interests, had long fought off. In order to be as responsive as possible to the community, I worked with a group of citizens comprising all parties, reporting constantly to them and securing from them proposals for measures, views on pending legislation and suggestions for improving my work. I established an office in Harlem; Pete had a similar headquarters in Brooklyn. I know of no other councilmen who offered such facilities to the public.

"Servicing" the public meant that my office was open to all citizens in connection with their individual problems. During my six years in the council, I must have personally interviewed or handled the problems of some 10 to 15 thousand persons. They had serious problems, generally involving the basic necessities of food, shelter and clothing—with jim-crow aggravating the family misery. Almost invariably they were pathetic or tragic. Sometimes I could do nothing more than permit a mother whose son had been a victim of unjust police action to unburden her troubled soul. Very often young couples would come to be married. I would have to inform them, regretfully, that a city councilman did not have the power to perform a marriage ceremony.

Of the individual problems, perhaps the largest was discrimination in employment and housing. Many apartments were found for possibly one in ten homeless citizens, but jobs were more difficult. Some Negro and white workers were placed through the trade unions, which were happy to cooperate with my office.

Once a Negro mother came to my office in tears. Her son was an American soldier who had spent a year-and-a-half overseas. He had been returned to Illinois under court-martial and dishonorably discharged from the army. We investigated the case and found that his offense was that he had protested a partic-

---

*Evidently, this was a "crime"—and it was one of the prime reasons for the defeat of Proportional Representation in 1947, and for the three-party gang-up against me in the 1949 campaign.

ularly brutal instance of jim-crow mistreatment. We carried on
several weeks of correspondence with the army authorities, finally
cutting through several miles of red tape. We were agreeably
surprised when, several months later, we were notified that his
case had been reconsidered and that he had been given an honorable discharge. We were as happy as his mother.

Once I was able to intercede with the Board of Health to have
a vaccine station permit issued to a white neighborhood druggist.
Though Harlem was the most congested area of the city, it had
fewer such stations, or hospital and other health facilities, than
any other section of the city. Harlem Hospital, the sole city institution catering to the general public, had 400 beds—for a population of 600,000! The hospital was known in Harlem as the
"butcher shop"—no reflection on the doctors and nurses who,
overworked and in second-grade facilities, were trying to keep
up with a staggering burden of cases. The countless unnecessary
deaths that took place in that medical factory might well be
charged to the city of New York, since it could find no money
for providing adequate hospital facilities for the people of
Harlem.

To be sure, there were other hospitals in Harlem—in the
midst of the Negro sections. But they did not accept Negro pa-
tients—no matter how grave their illness. One of the most shocking instances of this brutal discrimination was the case of W. C.
Handy's wife, who died a few minutes after she had been refused
admittance to a lily-white hospital in the center of Negro Harlem.

As I began my first term in the council, I had one regret—I
would have less time to devote to the functioning of the party
and to organizational tasks among the workers. I had to miss
many important meetings of party committees, although my
comrades did everything possible to accommodate the time of
meetings to the council obligations of Pete and myself. As a
result, my council work suffered, and so did my party work—not
to mention my own Marxist education. Just as I could not have
been elected without the party, I could not adequately fulfill my
official obligations without it. I confess I preferred party work to
any public office. That was why I had given up the practice of

law 11 years earlier. But knowing the needs and demands of the movement as a whole, I laid aside my personal preference.

The associations one forms, by necessity, in public office are sometimes revolting, seldom rewarding and nearly always politically unsanitary and unwholesome. One has to be careful not to absorb these associations even by osmosis and it is most interesting that the arrogant bourgeois politicians think we should be tickled to rub shoulders with them. The capitalists pay us a big compliment when they assume that one Communist in an organization of tens of thousands can influence the entire body, but that the same thousands can never influence one real Communist. It is a compliment that we Communists—being human—do not always deserve, and of course it is not meant as a tribute but as a slander. Actually, the slander is more against the thousands in the organization, who are treated as incapable of thinking for themselves, than it is of the Communists. We do not possess any such supernatural powers. When we are persuasive it is because of the truth and correctness of our contentions. If they are not true—then why jail us and persecute us?—the American people will see their untruth, as they have been able through the years to ultimately puncture falsehood.

One of the bills I introduced proposed the outlawing of jim-crow in the infamous Stuyvesant Town housing project. The measure provided for the withdrawal of the tax-exemption privilege from any landlord or realty owner who discriminated in the selection of tenants. One of the targets of the measure was the Metropolitan Life Insurance Company, whose president had declared publicly that no Negro tenant would be allowed to dwell in the project. The state legislature had passed a housing redevelopment law (under which Stuyvesant Town was built) which left a loophole big enough to permit the whole confederate army to pass through. The bill I introduced was designed to plug this loophole. Actually, it was introduced jointly by Councilman Stanley M. Isaacs, a Republican, and myself. His efforts in its behalf were able and conscientious, and I was happy to be co-sponsor with him.

The Mayor had a sensitivity on this issue which virtually drove him into a tantrum at the very mention of Stuyvesant Town. It was as though he realized he had made a political mistake, but couldn't turn back for fear of losing face. It was his whip that had jammed the discriminatory contract through the Board of Estimate. He deserved his share of the blame, but neither Governor Dewey nor the Tammany Democrats did one thing to prevent the city's ratification of the contract, nor aided one bit in the campaign to pass the Isaacs-Davis bill.

This bill was the most important one I introduced in my first term. For the measure would have seriously dented a powerful unwritten landlord rule in New York City—that white apartment houses, residential areas and neighborhoods must be barred to Negro Americans.

Pete and I introduced other legislation—Pete granting me joint sponsorship on many of the measures he had ably worked out and introduced in the first term. As a matter of fact, some 14 measures I had sponsored were passed by the council—a record that compared favorably with that of any other councilman.

Notwithstanding the overwhelming support for the Isaacs-Davis Bill, the Tammany majority stalled, hemmed and hawed. For a solid year they conducted a silent filibuster. They continually raised the smokescreen alibi that the measure was unconstitutional. They were all for it, but the courts "would not uphold it." Of course, the chief opponent of the bill was the Metropolitan, one of the biggest landowners in the United States, with vast plantation and farm holdings in the deep South, as well as immense realty holdings in New York. Its assets (according to the *New York Times* of February 21, 1952) made it the second largest corporation in the world—second only to AT&T. It was an empire, not a corporation. This was the prime colossus we had to contend with in attempting to pass the Isaacs-Davis bill. Add to this the real estate lobby—a powerful combination which aimed to maintain intact the rigid segregation of Negroes and Porto Ricans—and it is easy to see what we were up against.

After Tammany's majority had been raising its bogus arguments of unconstitutionality until early 1945, the public pressure

forced them to execute a maneuver. They did not enact the
Isaacs-Davis bill. Instead, the majority leader, Sharkey, took our
bill and wrote another just like it—in all but one particular.
The bill he wrote, which was later enacted, actually left jim-crow
in Stuyvesant Town untouched. It penalized jim-crow in future
tax-exempt private projects, that is, from 1945 on (Stuyvesant
Town had been authorized in 1943). We had won an important
skirmish, but we had lost the battle. The billion-dollar Metropolitan was bigger than the elected legislative body of eight million New York citizens.

The struggle brought forth many by-products. Not the least
of these was the attempt of the Metropolitan to buy off the
Negroes' opposition to discrimination in Stuyvesant Town. It
announced, and subsequently built, another project under the
Housing Redevelopment Law, with tax exemption, called River-
ton. This was in Harlem. But the maneuver failed, because Negroes, fully conscious of the law that had been foisted on them,
insisted that white tenants be integrated into the house. They
were integrated, and at the same time the struggle against Stuyvesant Town went on unabated. Soon the tenants took it up.
One of them subleased an apartment to a Negro family, robbing
the Metropolitan completely of the argument that none of the
white tenants wanted Negroes in the project with them. The
Metropolitan sought to oust every white tenant who opposed
jim-crow in the project. Professor Lee Lorch, formerly of City
College, was driven from his faculty posts in New York, Phila-
delphia and finally from Fisk University. It wasn't until redoubled
public pressure made itself felt that the Metropolitan was compelled (in 1952) to withdraw its eviction proceedings against the
handful of tenants who had dared to defy its imperial sway.

Actually, the first bill passed under my own sponsorship turned
out to be the designation of Negro History Week as an official
annual observance of the city. It was proclaimed each year by
the Mayor and the city council for six years—the duration of
my membership in that body. Negro History Week had been
inaugurated 35 years before by the Association for the Study of
Negro Life and History, under the leadership of Carter G. Wood-

son, a brilliant, self-made scholar. It was to acclaim and revive the great contributions of the Negro people to the building of democracy—contributions buried in the pages of prejudiced American history textbooks. If this is true in New York, one can scarcely imagine the extent of the malignant falsifications of history in such states as Mississippi, South Carolina and Georgia. From my earliest recollection in the schools of Dawson and Atlanta, I was always keenly conscious of the Ku Klux versions of Negro history shoved under my nose. The least I could do as a member of the city council was to strike a blow against these slanders of my people.

The significance of the city council's action was greater than the formal observance. The resolution itself was a simple document recalling in broad terms the important contributions of the Negro in the fields of science, art, culture, industry and statesmanship—connecting these contributions with current history and calling upon the city and all its departments to collaborate with the Association in appropriately observing Negro History Week.*

Thus the city was officially on record for this observance—but only in form. I worked out and submitted appropriate activities

---

*The idea of the resolution had been worked out in close coordination with the local Harlem branch of the Association for the Study of Negro Life and History. The latter gave an annual breakfast at which, as a regular item, I was called upon to make a few remarks and to read the council resolution and the Mayor's proclamation. Twice I read the proclamations of Mayor La Guardia and three times of Mayor O'Dwyer. The sixth time, which fell in February 1949, in the midst of my Smith Act trial, I was not invited to participate in the annual breakfast. The interesting thing about this is that the city council had felt compelled to pass the annual resolution, although I was in the midst of a trial for "conspiracy to teach and advocate the overthrow of the government by force and violence." I remember vividly the day the resolution was passed in 1949. The federal court was just across the street from the council chamber in City Hall. At about 4 PM Judge Medina and Prosecutor McGohey called me and my co-defendants "menaces to society." At 5 PM I walked across the street to City Hall where the council straightaway passed the resolution on Negro History Week, sponsored and introduced by a "menace to society."

for the schools, the various city departments and officials. I conducted a year-round campaign against prejudiced textbooks in
the schools. Some of these were so crass that they were removed
after I had quoted merely a few passages from them in a letter
to the department of education. And I called these to the attention of the Mayor and Superintendent of Schools during Negro
History Week. But it was of little use. They were not really
interested in the warping of children's minds by racist history
books.

But the city of New York now had an official tradition of
observing Negro History Week, and the observation was picked
up later by the state government. It is something the people of
New York can be proud of—even though they have never been
encouraged to make full use of it by the municipal administration. Such tributes as are deserved in connection with the event
should be paid to the Negro people, to several progressive organizations, and to many advanced CIO and AFL trade unions.

Another of the struggles we waged was around discrimination
in the Fire Department. It had been brought to my attention
that Negro members of the various fire companies were assigned
to special beds in the fire houses. White firemen, in between
calls, could occupy any beds in the building, but Negro firemen
were relegated to "Negro beds." They were also denied certain
kinds of promotions. One Negro in the department had risen to
batallion chief and was pointed to as an answer to all complaints
of discrimination.

The city council refused to pass my resolution condemning
such practices, but only agreed to enact a resolution to investigate the complaint through a special hearing. I conferred with
the Negro firemen and we decided to accept the change from
"condemnation" to "investigation"—confident that the facts exposed would force an improvement in conditions. The city council
majority preferred an investigation because they anticipated
hopefully that none of the Negro firemen would show up to
testify—for fear of losing their jobs. Hints of reprisal against
those who did appear filled the air.

But the Negro firemen, a militant and intelligent group,

showed up with bells on. They were solid as rock, and they burned with the kind of fire—the fire of the struggle for justice and dignity—that couldn't be put out. They jeopardized their jobs, their seniority and tenure rather than be intimidated. They made a powerful and impressive appearance—surprising the Tammany majority on the committee. There were about 40 of them—the committee room was jammed; the reporters from City Hall press room, hearing there was to be a big show, hung from the rafters.

Actually the Tammany majority had openly and shamelessly sabotaged the hearing but it had not turned out as they expected. They had asked the head of the Fire Department to appear to refute the charges, hoping to whitewash the department in the absence of the firemen themselves. The chief came, along with other high-placed officials, but the Negro firemen were there, too, in force.

When the hearing began, a question from me drew a promise from the Fire Chief that there would be no reprisals against the firemen who testified. It was the custom of the city council to permit the mover of a resolution to conduct the hearings. But the majority would scarcely permit me to get a word in edgewise. They tried the pettiest of tricks to bar my participation, even to the point of claiming I wasn't impartial. Few people were fooled —least of all the Negro firemen. They took the stand one after another, revealing the details of the humiliating discrimination existing in the department.

The hearing was a success, even though the council subsequently smothered my resolution. The facts of discrimination got to the people—partly through the press—and a short while later the jim-crow bed system was abolished and other reforms were instituted. And there were no reprisals. The system of jim-crow did not come to an end, although it received a few good whacks through our action.

The Fire Department entered my life again later when I started my own investigation of the reason for so many fires in Harlem—more fires than in any other residential area. Then I found that there were fewer fire houses per population than in any other area of the city. This accounted for the devastation wreaked by the fires—the sparsely distributed apparatus was too far away to get to the scene in time. I found that the engines took a longer time to arrive at fires in Harlem than they did in any other part of the city.

My investigation also showed that the business section and the exclusive residential areas, in addition to having a higher percentage of well-placed fire-fighting equipment, also had a system of double water outlets, whereas even single systems were scarce in Harlem. The council did not attempt to refute the facts, which were undeniable. Their answer revealed the most cynical disregard for human life I had ever heard. It hit me with such force that I shall never forget it—revealing how cheap the Negro's life was in their eyes. . . .

It was inevitable that a sense of frustration—of being fenced in—should occasionally arise in one who took seriously his membership in the council. The council was powerless to legislate on matters pertaining to the school system and to other areas of vital importance to the welfare of the people. Consequently, it was necessary to resort frequently to resolutions—which might cover subject-matter from a local parade to the biggest question of foreign policy. When Pete and I introduced such resolutions, they were dubbed "Communist propaganda"; when the Tammany councilmen introduced them, it was "American statesmanship." Ours were usually defeated; theirs were almost invariably passed.

Nevertheless, after many bitter debates, four of my resolutions were passed during the latter part of my first term. There were two on FEPC, one urging the adoption of a national FEPC and the other urging adoption of a state FEPC. Another placed the city of New York on record as urging congress to pass a national anti-poll tax bill—a measure designed to enfranchise six million whites and four million Negroes in seven poll-tax states.

A fourth was passed early in 1945, at the height of the struggle to break down the iron curtain against Negroes in big league baseball. This movement had reached tremendous proportions in New York and, to a certain extent, throughout the country.

The trade union movement took it up in a big way and so did millions of white baseball fans and progressives. Many big league baseball players expressed support, thereby depriving the baseball magnates of the bogus contention that white players would not play on the same team with Negro players. This movement resulted in a nonpartisan citizens' committee, ranging all the way from La Guardia and O'Dwyer to myself.

We found that the baseball magnates were holding their annual meeting in New York at the Vanderbilt Hotel, and we greeted them with a big demonstration in front of the hotel, while an elected delegation went upstairs to wait on the magnates. I was one of the delegation of six, and Paul Robeson was another—voted by all of us to be our spokesman. No one had a better right to speak for American sports than he—he had been chosen on Walter Camp's All-American football team repeatedly; he had been a four-letter man at Rutgers; a semi-pro baseball, football and basketball star. Paul had fulfilled the aspirations of every American boy—white, as well as Negro.

Paul gave the baseball tycoons a lesson in American sportsmanship. They knew Paul spoke for a whole people and for millions of white baseball fans. But they were too shrewd to admit their own responsibility for the ban against Negro players. They hemmed and hawed about it being "difficult to find qualified Negro players," and about "not pressing the issue too fast—it must be done gradually." They used all the well-known clichés.

Paul easily demolished their arguments. His antagonists were conscious of the significance of the occasion. Baseball, the "great American pastime," was on the spot. They finally told us they had no objection in principle and they would hire the first qualified Negro. Their concession was filled with ifs, ands and buts, and it did not quiet the protest. In the midst of the struggle, my resolution was introduced and, after some watering down to save the faces of the Yankee, Giant and Dodger owners, it passed.

Subsequently, the Dodgers purchased Jackie Robinson from a Negro ball club. A small reception was given for him in New York—attended by about 25 trade union, Negro, progressive and

Communist leaders. Paul and I were present. He commended Robeson for his contributions to the struggle and said a few kind words to me on the city council resolution which, he said, he had learned about on the West Coast. We were happy because we felt he was aware of the long struggle put up by his own people and by the labor and progressive movement to achieve this symbolic triumph. Alas, when the political atmosphere changed, so did Jackie Robinson. He soon forgot that it was the struggles of the people—his own, in the first place—that put him where he was.

Early in 1944, I was the recipient of several citations. One came to me on the national Negro History Week radio broadcast in January—as the first Negro Communist to become a member of an elected legislative body in the United States. A similar citation came from the *Pittsburgh Courier*. And later a citation at a *New Masses* banquet, where Charles Drew, the distinguished Negro scientist and surgeon, was also cited for his contributions to the development of the American blood bank during World War II—during which, incidentally, the blood of Negroes was segregated. I remember this occasion vividly, for it was the last time I saw or talked with Drew prior to his accidental death in 1951. We had been personal friends and had a strong respect for each other since our school days at Amherst, when we played side by side on the football team. His death was a tragic loss to science and society, and it affected me deeply.*

The years 1944-45 proved to be a fateful period for me in particular and for the American Communist movement in general. In the city council, Cacchione and I continued to press for progressive legislation and reforms of a democratic character. But soon the incorrect direction in which the party was moving cast its shadow over our council endeavors. Mistakes were made, some of them serious.

Nevertheless, it was a mixed period, in which certain reforms

---

*Efforts to obtain special permission to attend his funeral in Washington, D.C., were unavailing. The Federal District Court in New York would not temporarily relax my bail restrictions even for this purely personal feeling of sorrow over the death of a life-long friend.

were achieved and in which mistakes did not reveal themselves too glaringly. One of the most important of these reforms was the successful struggle for a New York State FEPC. The federal FEPC, established by President Roosevelt under pressure, had been so belabored, attacked and starved for funds that its effectiveness had been seriously hampered. As a result, there arose in dozens of states and localities demands for state FEPC's to supplement the national organization. Nowhere was this demand more insistent than in New York. Governor Dewey tried as long as he could to ignore it, but he was compelled to change his direction in midstream. He set up a commission of prominent citizens to investigate. The whole world knew that New York was riddled with discrimination, and this was obviously an empty gesture on Dewey's part. Set up in the latter part of 1943, the commission was to report to the state legislature in 1944. But the wily governor would not permit the commission to report in 1944, and the chance of passing the law was lost.

A storm of protest fell upon the governor's head. Members of the commission resigned publicly in disgust. It was no mystery why Dewey was temporizing with the FEPC issue. He was running for president, and at that moment he had his emissaries in the deep South lining up Southern Republican convention delegates. . . . Dewey went down to a smashing defeat. I doubt if he carried a Negro precinct in the whole North. The Negro voters of Harlem helped to bury him.

Nothing is more effective with a reactionary than a good beating at the hands of the people. Still running for president, Dewey changed his tactics. He maneuvered to make partisan capital out of the movement instead of bucking it. He contrived to take the play away from the Democrats, making his side-kick, Republican State Senator Irving Ives, the sponsor of the proposed FEPC law —known as the Ives-Quinn bill.

The hearing on this measure was conducted so that Dewey's friends were given first opportunity to speak. This was in order to give them the best press and also to keep to the end the most militant speakers—those who were most responsible for the measure. They hoped by then the crowd would be gone and that the morning editions of the press would have gone to bed. But virtually the whole crowd stayed; trade-union, Negro and other militant forces demanded the right to be heard. The hearing lasted until late at night; it had begun at 10 AM that morning—it was a magnificent victory, after a struggle that lasted a year and a half.

While I spoke at the hearing, my main job had been to help others gather and organize the New York contingent. My councilmanic office was turned into an organizing center for the delegation. It was well disciplined and well prepared.

The incorrect policies that underlay certain aspects of my work in the city council were not so easily discernible in the waging of the FEPC struggle and other reforms for which we pressed in the city council. But in other instances it was not at all difficult to recognize.

There is no such thing as a politician without a line. It is either the people's line or the bosses' line. I, as a Communist, considered public office as an instrumentality for helping to effect the will of the working class—whose ultimate destination is the socialist transformation of society. My membership in the Communist Party and my Marxist convictions were not incidental to, but were the source of, my usefulness to the people who elected me. To discard them as bourgeois politicians shake off their campaign promises would be like cutting off my hand. When, therefore, I failed to adhere to my Marxist principles, I made many mistakes—of omission as well as commission. Of these, two were outstanding: the first, when I voted to support a sales tax levy—a tax always heaviest upon the working people; the second, when I voted to extend the term of city councilman from two to four years. A third mistake—not as fundamental as the first two—was my vote for the anti-discrimination housing law, in spite of the fact that it did not ban discrimination in Stuyvesant Town—which had been the main object of the Isaacs-Davis bill.

Opposition to sales taxes is a matter of principle for the working class—to a worker it constitutes a wage-cut. Mayor La Guardia had proposed the sales tax levy in 1944. The tax had first been imposed during the depression, and proceeds were to be earmarked for relief purposes. Like most taxes on the poor, it had remained, even though it had been supposed to last only as long as the depression-relief emergency. Still other reasons were given for continuing the tax—the subway operating deficit, hospitals, schools, etc. The arguments were indeed persuasive, especially since the tug-o'-war between the city and the state on financial questions invariably left New York the short end of the stick.

As a matter of fact, when the vote came in the city council, Pete and I refused to vote for it. Whereupon, the majority refused to put the question to a vote, and a debate ensued. The majority leader declared that unless the minority—including the Communist members—took responsibility for the sales tax also, it would not be passed and the city would be left without adequate revenues. Cacchione and I refused to budge—Sharkey's bellowing was patently fraudulent. The council took a recess for an hour or more. Pete and I conferred together. Meanwhile, we were deluged with almost tearful pleas from the Mayor's spokesmen. It was an extraordinary procedure—none like it before and none since. Finally, Pete and I reasoned that since we were part of a broad coalition of forces, including the La Guardia administration, we should go along with the sales tax, even though we were opposed to it in principle. The council was recalled into session. We then voted "aye."

We thought we had been wrong, and were very anxious to discuss the matter with other party leaders. But, much to our surprise, they thought we had been wrong in delaying our vote so long. It later developed that the agreement of these comrades only signified that they, too, were injected with the same un-Marxist virus as we were. The truth is we were right the first time, and should never have changed our votes even if hell froze over.

Neither Pete nor I ever learned to like what we had done, but we consoled ourselves with the explanation that it fitted in with the "new line of the party." Little did we know at that time that it was precisely the new line of the party that was off the beam.

And this was the case with regard to the proposal to lengthen the term of city councilmen from two to four years. It was argued that the short term did not provide enough time to achieve substantial legislative programs. These contentions did not influence Cacchione and me. Yet we went along with the proposal. We had to find reasons of our own. We had no difficulty finding them in the "new line of the party." The reasoning was that we were now a part of a broad anti-fascist progressive coalition, whose political leader was Franklin D. Roosevelt and whose political instrument was the Democratic Party. If this was true on a national scale, why not on a municipal scale? The new line projected a long term of working-class collaboration and alliance with the Democratic Party. What better than dovetailing our own party's electoral activities with those of the local Democrats—thus eliminating the councilmanic fight against Tammany midway in the mayoralty term, and going along with them every four years, at the end of each mayoralty term.

The reasons for the four-year term proposal and the enthusiasm of the Democrats were scarcely to be found in the innocent arguments for it. It may be that La Guardia did intend to save campaign money by a joint ticket every four years, but the total sum was hardly worth mentioning. A four-year term meant two years more of gravy and graft; extending the term made the municipal government less responsive to the people. A weakness of the Charter was that it gave the council power to perpetuate itself in office without the people's having a say. The extension of a term could be accomplished by a simple majority vote of the councilmen.

My third lapse—with respect to the Isaacs-Davis bill—affected its main objective, the end of discrimination in Stuyvesant Town. If this had been accomplished, automatically it would have barred discrimination in all future housing. To be sure, the Democrats stole our bill and in doing so they left out its guts. That fact alone was sufficient for me to have refrained from supporting it—or, at the least, I should have refrained from voting. Again the influence of the new line reared its head. The measure —even without outlawing discrimination in Stuyvesant Town—

was progressive. And since the Democrats in the city council were the local voice of the political party with which we contemplated a long-term alliance, it followed that we should second the progressive measures they recommended. But this was form without content. It was not a vote for continued struggle—although the struggle did continue, including my own participation in it. It was primarily a vote of collaboration—if what was right couldn't be gotten, then go along with what could be gotten. This did not reflect a correct role for the independent party of the working class.

It goes almost without saying that none of these mistakes appeared as such at the time they were made. I had no intention of departing from the scientific principles of Marxism-Leninism. As a matter of fact, I thought I was upholding them. Further, a Communist does not oppose reforms obtained in the framework of capitalism. But in voting for the sales tax and the other measures, I had voted against the economic and democratic interests of the working class. This was objectively true—whatever my intentions and even though these votes conformed to the line of the party.

A word about the new line of the party, which had crystallized and congealed as the official line at the National Convention in May 1944. It was called the Teheran policy and was based upon a book by Earl Browder, presenting postwar domestic and international perspectives. Stripped of its pseudo-Marxist verbiage, the book was based upon a diplomatic document signed by Roosevelt, Churchill and Stalin at Teheran. From that meeting, it drew the erroneous conclusion that capitalism had overcome its inherent cyclical crises, that monopoly capitalism would grow gradually into socialism, that the trusts and monopolies of the United States would lead this country and the world into a warless, secure and prosperous life—without exploitation and oppression. Hence, a Communist Party was not necessary and was liquidated into an amorphous Communist Political Association. Its members were to join political parties; they would find their place preferably in the Democratic Party.

All this was, of course, total subservience to the capitalist class, complete subordination to its bourgeois liberal wing, then under the leadership of F.D.R. Fortunately, our party was able to arrest this debacle before it reached its logical conclusion. Only Browder and a half-dozen others ended up in the swamp.

My individual responsibility could not be dismissed. I was not only a member of the council; I was also a party leader, and the Teheran line and perspective had been formulated with my participation. When at the May 1944 National Convention of the party, this policy was officially adopted, I not only voted for the policy but accepted full responsibility for carrying it out.

When Communists make mistakes, however, they disclose them, analyze them, seek their source, try to correct them and then establish guarantees against their recurrence. All of this is done publicly. This is the hallmark of a serious Marxist party and has no counterpart in any other political organization. Thus, the erroneous policy was exposed and discussed, and corrective guarantees were adopted in a special emergency party convention in July 1945. A fuller account of this period can be found in the documentary history contained in publications of the party and made available at the time. I will not dwell on it further in these pages, except to say that the struggle against the Teheran line was stubbornly and courageously conducted by William Z. Foster, and that, on the basis of Foster's polemic against Browder's book *Teheran,* Jacques Duclos, a French Communist leader wrote an article in the official organ of the French Communist Party demolishing the Browder line.

The false character of the Teheran line is implicit today, as American monopoly capitalism leads the world toward catastrophic war, keeping its productive machine from cyclical collapse by prodigious war expenditures—with the blood of Americans and Asians. . . .

My first term in the council ended December 31, 1945. The election for the next term, however, took place a month earlier. The Negro Labor Victory Committee in Harlem, which had played a decisive role in unifying the Negro masses in support of the war against Hitlerism, was the core of the Negro-labor-progressive coalition. Backing my candidacy, it sent an open letter to the Democratic and Republican parties demanding that they both give me the councilmanic designation as the overwhelming choice of the community. Soon afterwards I received word from Tammany Hall that it was considering naming me as the Democratic Party candidate from Harlem. I knew of the request of the Negro Labor Committee and its wide influence among the Negro people but, for a thousand-and-one reasons, I did not consider that a Democratic nomination was possible for me.

Nevertheless, at a subsequent conference with several Democratic County leaders, I realized that the proposed designation was serious. It was agreed that I would register as a Democrat, that I would retain my Marxist convictions and affiliations, and that I would receive the Democratic designation. I confess I felt a bit strange at first, even though this was in line with the Teheran perspective of the party. Since I was at that time a member of the Communist Political Association, which was nonpartisan and not a political party, I not only could join another political party, it was my duty to do so—especially since the Democratic Party was the main political instrument of the Roosevelt coalition. I registered Democratic.

At a rally at the Golden Gate, where my candidacy was projected, the Democratic Party County Committee announced that it had accorded me its designation and I made a few remarks of acceptance. It was the worst speech I had ever made. It was obvious to me—if not to the filled auditorium—that I was not ideologically adjusted to the change. The applause of the audience was desultory. It was as if my neighbors and co-workers in Harlem did not know whether to laugh or to cry, to be happy or to mourn. Actually it was a time to weep—not over me, but over the fact that the Communists were lowering their colors.

This ceremony occurred on a Sunday; the next morning scare headlines appeared in the papers. The majority, led by the Hearst and Scripps-Howard publications, screamed, "Democrats give nomination to Red." For ten days the radio commentators and the press screamed as if the revolution had come. The

Democratic majority in the city council was stunned. One could hear the taunts from the Republicans and other minority members: "So now Davis, the Communist, is a member of the majority. When is he moving over to your side?" The Democrats said nothing. I, in the middle, enjoyed their short-lived discomfiture. For a brief interlude they were on the receiving end of red-baiting.

Soon the press and the die-hard political leaders were joined in their hysteria by "50th Street"—the headquarters of the Catholic hierarchy. What was the godly Democratic Party coming to, they screamed, giving its hallowed designation to a godless, Moscow-serving Communist? The reporters were chasing me around, insisting on statements of one sort or another. I escaped them and blandly ignored the press. When the time came to speak, I would do so in no uncertain terms.

Finally, the issue, which began to overshadow all others in the pre-election jockeying, could no longer be sidestepped by William O'Dwyer—whose lifelong ambition it was to become mayor. He was about to be the unanimous choice of the Democratic machines in the five boroughs, when along came this Communist issue. The worst part of it was that he wasn't in a clash with me or the Communists—he was in a head-on tussle with the Manhattan Tamanny section of his own party, which had designated me. That he didn't like. And I wouldn't oblige him, or pull his chestnuts out of the fire by entering the fray. I played it cool. Let the Democrats fight it out among themselves. In a sense, Tammany had made one decent nomination in its modern history; unaccustomed to this, it was about to wreck the party and Mr. O'Dwyer's ambitions.

After about nine days, the papers began to hint of special conferences between O'Dwyer and Spellman at 50th Street. Two days later the papers carried the story that O'Dwyer was under terrific pressure. On the one hand, he needed the left-wing, trade union and Negro sectors of the coalition and did not want to offend them by denouncing my nomination. On the other hand, he did not wish to offend the old-line clerical-fascist wing of the Democratic Party—the Jim Farleys, Spellmans, and Hearst-Roy

Howard papers. What to do? O'Dwyer must have had some sleepless nights communing with the infinite.

Finally he came out of it. The power of 50th Street, of the monopoly press, of the ultra-reactionaries who dominated the Tammany machine was too much for him. He capitulated. The papers published the story: O'Dwyer had laid down an ultimatum to Tammany Hall; either it withdrew my nomination or he wouldn't run. It didn't take Tammany long to decide what to do—with the whole pro-fascist pack on its heels; it withdrew my nomination.

But this, too, had to be done skillfully or else Tammany would run pell-mell into a resentful Harlem, into a disillusioned Negro population throughout the city. Now it had to figure out a way of withdrawing the nomination from the "overwhelming choice" of only a few days ago. It declared that since I had reaffirmed my Communist convictions publicly after receiving the nomination, the Democratic designation had been withdrawn. The tempest in a teapot was over.

The howlers for blood, however, did not stop there. Once the Democratic designation was withdrawn from me, they demanded that Tammany put another Negro in the race to defeat me. Otherwise, they said the Democrats would be assumed to be secretly supporting me. And Tammany complied. Thus, in the space of two weeks I had run the gauntlet from the "overwhelming choice" to one who must be defeated at all costs. To accomplish this task, the Tammany committee designated Ruth Whitehead Whaley, a Negro woman whose sole qualification was that she had won some elocution prizes many years before. Actually, she was still in a deep sleep, politically speaking. Needless to say, Mrs. Whaley was snowed under.

This whole episode had occurred early in the corrective and self-critical process taking place in the party. I was so occupied in this all-decisive process that all of my political activities became somewhat disoriented. However, it did not take me and other party leaders long to recognize that I had been off the beam. The brief flirtation with Tammany was, and will forever remain, a nightmare. This underestimation of the influence and strength of monopoly capital is the biggest and most serious I had ever committed. It is not altogether surprising that this kind of error happens. It grows out of the tendency to revert to the fallacious theory of "American exceptionalism"—that American capitalism is different, stronger, above the laws of social development. . . .

My second term in the City Council was to be a stormy one. Mayor LaGuardia said as much when he swore me in for the second time. "Davis," he said, after administering the oath of office, "you're going to have tough sledding this time."

"Communists prepare for all eventualities," I answered. He smiled. It is quite possible that we had entirely different things in our minds. I had in mind the correction of our party's policy at the Emergency National Convention in July, six months before I was sworn in. I knew that with the re-constitution of the party as the independent political party of the working class on sound Marxist-Leninist principles under William Z. Foster's leadership there was no ground for unrealistic expectations. And I was prepared. I had learned from the personal experience I had had with the Tammany Democrats. In this sense, Pete and I were prepared for the worst, though never ceasing to work for the best.

Incidentally, Mayor La Guardia, who kept abreast of the Communist Party's policy on current issues, called me to his office one day to give him the "low-down" on the meaning of our Emergency Party Convention. I started to explain, but there were so many interruptions that we didn't finish. He never got around to it again before he left office.

I could have told him that our organization had been re-established as the independent political party of the working class. It was this historic step which enabled the Communists and those who respected them to stand for peace and democracy against the howling storms of war incitement and reaction which struck the country in the dark years that followed. In the process, I had learned a qualitatively new approach to Marxist theory and activity—which would improve my ability to serve the people as a member of the city council of New York.

CHAPTER EIGHT

DEATH OF MY FATHER

Late in October 1945, two weeks before election day, my father died. It was a blow such as I had not sustained since the death of my mother in 1932. My grief was only partially cushioned by my absorption in the election campaign.

My father died in Harlem Hospital, of cancer complicated by a severe heart ailment. He was close to 75 and the suffering he endured carried him away because his weak heart could not stand the debilitating process of the other dread disease.

I had seen him only a few hours before he died, thinking there was a chance he could live a while longer. He had said: "Son, I hope I can stay alive until you're re-elected, but it's going to be hard to do it." These were his last words to me.

I had never seen my father in such a weakened state—his voice was scarcely audible. I had known him only as a strong personality with an iron constitution and a powerful voice.

His funeral took place in Atlanta, in Friendship Baptist Church, where he was a deacon and where 14 years earlier my mother was a member of the choir. He was buried beside my mother in Southview Cemetery in the family plot. My sister and I attended the funeral. I dropped everything and left the campaign to the party.

After his first heart attack in 1944, my sister and I tried to get him to live in New York with us, but he would have none of it. He would not move his home because Atlanta was the scene of the most fruitful part of his life—and some of the most stinging, bitter defeats. He lived alone with his memories, in sight of many of the monuments which he had helped to erect. There were a few old friends, the intangible ties with the past that bound him to a social and political setting that was rapidly disappearing. The changes that had taken place during the

145

Rooseveltian era came too late in his life for him to make the necessary adjustments.

All his life he had been an old-fashioned Republican. He had held high positions in the party, that is, for a Negro. He was a Republican of the Abe Lincoln-Frederick Douglass type. He felt that the Republican Party that had freed the Negroes from chattel slavery would free him from the fetters of jim-crow, disfranchisement and persecution which had replaced the manacles of human bondage. When, therefore, in the declining years of his life, he had begun to realize that this was not to be, he became bitterly disillusioned. Republican Party politics, in a sense, had been his life. He was a casualty of his illusions.

I had toward my father the filial attachment of any dutiful son. With it, I developed a deep respect for his high personal talents and abilities. Yet I was able to view him fairly objectively and even when I was quite young I had subjected his way of life to close scrutiny. This is a tendency I must have learned from him, for he maintained the same attitude toward me.

Apart from the ties that bound me to my father, I saw his life as a potentially fascinating chronicle. Many lessons could be drawn from it relating to the struggle for Negro liberation. He represented an earlier and different period of this struggle, but in some ways it had a profound effect upon the present situation.

My father, first of all, was a reformist, a firm believer in free enterprise, which, within the limitations of his being a Negro, did well by him personally. During his career he hovered somewhere between the Negro upper middle class and the small bourgeoisie; indeed, for many years he was quite wealthy. Within the framework of his reformist philosophy, he was a staunch believer in first-class citizenship for the Negro people, a vigorous and personally courageous opponent of disfranchisement and of the brutal oppression of his people. He was honest and could fight with the intensity of a crusader who was conscious of his destiny. He had an abiding faith in the common people, and his middle-class status never separated him from them. Indeed, he possessed a disdain for the Negro aristocracy— which was fully reciprocated.

My father was the idol of the backwoods poor Negro farmers, of the luckless disinherited city dwellers who felt the brunt of urban oppression in Atlanta, Birmingham, Nashville and other such centers. He was a brilliant organizer, a builder and a formidable foe, fearless and outspoken in his views, and willing to risk his life on issues involving the rights of Negroes. A powerful leader, he compelled the respect and even the fear of his adversaries—many of whom were Klansmen of the purest water.

Having had no formal education to speak of (perhaps to sixth grade), he was indeed a self-made man, possessing a great store of knowledge distilled from experience, environment and self-study. A man of generous impulses and high ambitions for himself, his family and his people, he more than met the standards of his day as a useful, constructive and patriotic citizen. The years of his peak were between 1910 and 1930.

As I have said elsewhere, father was pre-eminent in three fields—as a Negro fraternal order leader, as political leader and as editor and publisher of the Atlanta *Independent*. Under his leadership, the District Grand Order of the Odd Fellows, jurisdiction of Georgia, became the largest and wealthiest Negro fraternal organization in the South. The order built in 1912 the now famous Odd Fellows Block, fronting Auburn Avenue from Butler to Bell Streets in Atlanta. It consisted of a modern six-story office building and a two-story office annex housing a large auditorium which would seat about 2,000 persons. The auditorium later became the first modern movie house for Negroes in Atlanta. The Odd Fellows Building was the most up-to-date office structure owned by Negroes in the South for many years after erection. Its elevator and its automatic mail chute were then considered remarkable innovations. The whole block became the center around which the commercial and professional life of the Atlanta Negro community was built—it remains so to this date. It was subsequently pointed to dramatically by Booker T. Washington as the "way out" for the Southern Negro. His philosophy envisaged the advancement of the masses of Negroes by the development of a mercantile and even capitalist class. The joker, of course, was that for such a class to exist it could maintain itself only within the framework of, and at the sufferance of, the system of national oppression of the Negro. This was classic Negro reformism in its basic economic form.

The Odd Fellows block had been built with the nickels and dimes of Negro farmers, sharecroppers and workers, who paid for the policies of fraternal benefit insurance issued to each member by the society. It was based largely upon the rural Negro population, which lived under the worst kind of poll-tax, peonage and lynch law. As an expression of the national aspirations of the Negro people—aspirations most highly developed in the Black Belt—the Odd Fellows project had to be supported against the opposition of Southern white plantation owners, urban industrialists and other white supremacists who grudgingly watched its birth and growth. In fact, my father had manifested considerable daring, imagination and will power to carry it through. Often the Negro peasants who supported it were forbidden by Ku Klux plantation owners to join. But when the project was finished, the poverty-stricken Negro rural population was no better off economically, socially or politically. The Order for many economic and political reasons was doomed to failure. The 1929 depression gave it the *coup de grace*.

My father had viewed the society largely as a means of pooling the united strength of the Negro, of lifting his standard of living, of giving him dignity and ownership, of challenging the denial of his first-class citizenship. Such were his lofty motivations. But instinctively he had begun to realize the incompleteness of this course, and had combined his interest in the Order with politics. The focus of his attention was the Negro's right to vote. Once this was achieved, he felt, all other rights would fall into place automatically.

Born a few years after the Emancipation Proclamation, his mother a former slave (she died in 1922) and his brother, too, a former slave (he died in 1952), a reverential attachment to the Republican Party was bred into him, as was his hatred of the Democratic Party, which ruled the South. With his influential post in the Odd Fellows, he soon became the leader of the Republican Party in Georgia. The Odd Fellows became a

powerful Republican instrument. When he founded the Atlanta
Independent in 1903, it subsequently became a potent organ
for building the Society and the Republican Party. The paper
became famous all over Negro America for the fearlessness of
its editorial policy—especially on the issue of the franchise for
the Southern Negro. It was, during its heyday, easily the most
influential Negro weekly in the South. For many years, my
father was president of the National Negro Publishers Association—on the strength of the vigorous editorial policy of the
paper. I can remember during my earliest youth my father
saying that editorials are the "soul of a newspaper." If it has no
soul, he would continue, "it's not worth the paper it's printed
on." It made a positive and lasting impression upon me. My
father, in the role of editor and publisher of the *Independent*,
drew tremendous admiration, respect and family pride from me.

It was good that my father had this lofty appreciation of the
role of a newspaper, for it was always in the red. Sparse Negro
business enterprises were unable to support it with advertisements, and white capital wouldn't. It was a combination of an
Odd Fellows house organ and my father's interpretation of the
events of the day—plus his comments on contemporaries and
the burning issue of Negro rights. Other Negro weeklies were
more modern in appearance and broader in their coverage, but
their flabby editorial policies were hitched to their largest adver-
tisers. The *Independent* existed primarily on subscriptions and
on a subsidy from the Odd Fellows. As a youth in my teens,
when I went to Morehouse College, I spent a part of many
summer vacations as a subscription agent for the paper. But
even then—to say nothing of now—the newspaper industry was
so trustified that subscriptions alone could not keep a paper
alive. This, plus the failure of the Odd Fellows, the advent of the
depression, and other complications snuffed out the life of the
Independent. But during its life it had established for itself
a worthy and historical record. Just as it was admired and loved
by the Negro people, so it was hated by the Klan. In many
towns in Georgia it was not allowed. It was regarded, for example, in Swarnsboro, Georgia, as the *Daily Worker* is regarded

in the White House. For a Negro sharecropper to be caught reading the *Independent* in a jerkwater Georgia lynchtown was like waving a red flag before a bull.

I remember that my father once called me into his private office and showed me a big bundle of *Independents* that had been returned from a little town called Covington. A number of Odd Fellows—about 75 or 80 in all—subscribed to the paper. The bundle had been returned to Atlanta with scribbling on it from the white postmaster in Covington. It read: "Nigger Ben, we dont allow this paper in this town stirring up trouble among our niggers. Keep it out of here and stay out of here yourself."

I was about 16 but not too young to grasp the full meaning of this. My father patiently explained it to me. I was astounded and I suggested that my father do something about it. "What?" he asked. I replied that he should take the matter up with the Post Office Department, that the *Independent* possessed full second-class mailing privileges, that the postmaster was bound to deliver the papers, and so on. As a subscription "expert," I was well informed on the mailing rights of newspapers.

My father answered: "That's pretty good, son. But the post office is as bad as the postmaster in Covington." Then my eyes bulged when he told me what he was going to do about it.

"My son," he said, the way he would address me in moments of paternal warmth, "I have another plan. I'm going to Covington and I'm going to take copies of the *Independent* to give to anyone who'll take one."

"But, Dad," I said, "you're taking your life in your hands."

"This is the work of the Ku Klux Klan," he said, "and they're cowards. The worst thing you can do is to run away from them."

"But you're running after them," I said.

"No," he went on, "I'm only doing what any red-blooded American would do—white or black. I'm exercising my rights."

"That settles the matter then," I said.

"Not quite, I'm taking you with me. It will be a fine experience for you—the best way to learn."

I had the utmost admiration for my father in this role and

would have followed him to the end of the earth. Besides, the whole thing appealed to my youthful spirit of adventure.

Father decided to make the trip by auto and I drove him (about three weeks after he had discussed his intentions in the office).

He had had the Odd Fellows arrange a meeting in Covington on a Saturday afternoon about 2:00 PM. It was arranged in the Covington Courthouse—of all places. It was widely advertised with my father as principal speaker. The subject of his speech was the U.S. Constitution.

When we arrived, people were milling about the courthouse. Most of them were Negroes—sharecroppers and poor farmers— about 150 or 200. There were about 50 whites.

Father walked directly and boldly into and through the crowd, up the steps into the two-story brick courthouse building. He was surrounded by Negroes who had accompanied him inside. A group of white men followed him in. I was by his side. He went directly into the upstairs courtroom and the Negroes filed in behind him. I sat directly in front of him. He and two Negro residents of the town did not sit on the judge's bench but took their places on three chairs facing the audience, on the floor. The white people came in and stood around the walls with their hats on. The Negroes all removed their hats.

The atmosphere was fraught with expectancy. The silence was deafening. The place was filled to overflowing. The pockets of many of the whites bulged—but so did those of the Negroes.

I took the whole situation in at a glance, and I was nervously excited. My father was cool; if he wasn't, it certainly didn't show. Finally one of the local Odd Fellows, acting as chairman, got up and introduced my father as a leader of the Negro people, a believer in the Constitution and a real son of Georgia. It was not a flowery introduction—I doubt if the chairman had ever had one day of formal education—but it was an earnest and sincere one, uttered with the spirit of one saying, "here I take my stand."

My father rose to speak, and my heart was in my mouth. "Fellow-citizens," he began, "white and black. I am glad to see that my people respect this courthouse by removing their hats."

That was the challenge and my father had boldly chosen the issue—it was an audacious one. We looked around at the audience. Naturally, our eyes fell on the whites standing around the wall with their hats on. What would they do?

My father paused a full minute, awaiting the reaction to the blow he had struck. As he later explained, he wanted to see whether the whites hated the Negroes so much that they would not respect their own courthouse.

The next move was up to the badly outnumbered whites slumped along the walls. After about two minutes, one removed his hat. Then another followed suit. One of them walked out. Slowly and sullenly, as if they realized they were beaten, all who remained removed their hats.

The tension relaxed. My father went on speaking. He spoke for an hour about the Constitution, about the *Independent,* about the issues of the paper that had been returned to him, about the Negro's sufferings and his unrealized citizenship. He had them laughing and all but weeping. Even some of the whites—whom I watched almost as closely as the FBI watched me about 30 years later—cracked their tobacco-stained faces with a grin now and then.

When my father finished speaking, the atmosphere was normal. But no chances were taken—a group of about 20 Odd Fellows immediately surrounded him. One white man broke through to say, "Ben, I—God, that's the best speech I ever heard." My father, missing nothing, said: "I was just telling the truth. Here, take a copy of my paper." The startled white man took it, thanked my father and walked away.

Outside, the white group stood by themselves. Father walked up to them and handed each a copy of the Independent. As he walked away, one of them said: "He's the smartest nigger I ever saw. Didn't know they got so smart." I winced. The Odd Fellows escorted us to Dad's car. And we made our way back to Atlanta. The *Independent* built up an even bigger circulation in Covington afterwards.

On the way back, my father explained how the event had

been planned. He had written to one of the most reliable Negro organizers of the Odd Fellows, and members had come from three or four towns nearby; some were armed. The courthouse, according to local law and custom, was available for any patriotic meeting on the Constitution. No one really believed that my father would come—no one but the Odd Fellows. A defense committe had been set up to protect him in case of Klan violence. Some of the Odd Fellows remained outside as sentries.

It was a magnificent demonstration of the courage of the Negro farmers and, of course, my father's courage, and will remain undimmed in my memory. Such situations, to be sure, were not unusual for my father. He had experienced similar emergencies on many occasions. "You're lucky to be alive," I'd say when he told me about them, but he would always shrug it off, not regarding himself as a martyr at all.

Our home was always a kind of underground railroad. My mother would often get up in the middle of the night to fix a bed for a Negro sharecropper who had escaped from a Georgia peonage farm. They came to my father because they felt sure he would understand and would help. And he would—finding a job or a place to stay. I often told my father, after I became a Communist, that it was only the continuation of the role he had played in a different political period. But he would not concede that for a goodly number of years.

Along with Henry Lincoln Johnson and Robert Church, of Memphis, my father was a national figure in Republican Party politics. But their positions were largely of value only in the internal politics of the party. Negroes in the South could not vote in the national elections because of the poll tax, the white primary, grandfather clauses—and because of the rope and faggot. But my father and his friends were useful to the GOP for three reasons: First, they helped preserve the illusion that the Republicans were the party of the Negro in the deep South; then, it put the Democratic Party at a disadvantage, since it was their party which was the main instrument of oppression in the South. The GOP used this pretense of representation and this recognition of the Southern Negro as a way to gain the support of Northern Negroes, whose votes often constituted the balance of power. The votes of the Southern Negroes were important to aspirants for the GOP nominees for President. The Republicans were given an opportunity to pose as the party that gave representation to the Southern Negro. This hypocrisy had worked well from the time of the Civil War—until the master politician Roosevelt broke it up with the New Deal.

I can remember many convention fights my father waged, before the credentials committee of the Republican convention, against lily-white Georgia factions which sought to freeze Negroes out. I never knew him to lose one of these contests. But I also felt they were a mock battle to give the convention bosses a chance to appear as "friends of the Negro."

At the 1944 convention in Chicago, however, father, who was advocate for the black-and-tan faction, was called upon to use every resource at his command. And though he was loath to do it—as he later informed me—he resorted to the "Communist threat." He evidently hit the mark so well that newspapers throughout the country quoted this section of his speech as having won the day.

"For 50 years," he said, "I have been a Republican. I have supported the ticket and built the party—often at great personal expense. And now, for the first time, I see the seat of the Southern Negro in this convention in real jeopardy. . . . My son is now a member of the City Council of New York, elected on the Communist ticket. If this convention does not give us a seat, my people and I know where to go."

My father's "black-and-tan" faction was seated and the lily-white delegation rejected. It was father's valedictory address before the national Republican Party. In a certain personal sense, he handed the banner to me. May I keep it aloft! . . .

My father's record had showed him to be a brilliant and resourceful organizer and a resolute fighter. He was always at his best in the fight for others. When "Link" Johnson died—my father had helped elect him as the first National Committeeman in a Southern state since Reconstruction—my father became the candidate. After bitter struggles, he was elected, and, unlike his predecessors, he was going to stay in Atlanta to fulfill the duties of his post. Ominous threats developed from the Klan, the press and the most rabid of the white supremacists. (It could be tolerated that a Negro should be a national committeeman, as long as he stayed out of Georgia and did not exert his authority in person.)

On two different occasions the Klan burned crosses in our front yard. My father received threats through the mail and over the phone. For a month the windows in our home were stoned and broken. At night, the tires on my father's cars were cut to ribbons. When he appealed to the Atlanta police department, the chief told him he ought to give up the post to a white man and that would end the trouble. Later he assigned two policemen to our house, but this was only show. The terror and stoning continued —this time with police protection.

At that time I was away at Amherst. But I could follow these events in almost any newspaper—so flagrant were they. It was a virtual reign of terror. I naturally became very apprehensive about my parents. I wanted to return home until the fireworks were over. But my father reassured me by saying the situation was under control. Then I would read the next day of a fresh bombing attack.

The real casualty in the family was kept from me. My mother had been as resolute in staying at our Boulevard residence as my dad. In poor health, she had collapsed in the midst of this siege of violence. She had not been able to sleep or rest for days, and she never fully recovered from this assault upon her nerves. Afterwards her health deteriorated steadily, and six years later she died.

My father weathered the storm. When the Klan and its accomplices realized that he could not be intimidated, they gradually called off the terror. My father served several years as national committeeman, exercising every prerogative of the post, even down to okaying every postmaster and postmistress, every federal district attorney, every internal revenue collector, before they could get a presidential appointment—under the American patronage system as it was practiced. I used to view with sardonic pleasure the small town postmasters beating a path to my father's door—perhaps a Southern Klan-minded white seeking favors of a Negro political boss. I had a chance to see the shoe on the other foot for a spell—and the world did not come to an end.

When Hoover came into the White House, he figured that here was an opportunity to build the Republican Party in the South —to have a "two-party" system, with the most rabid white supremacists controlling both. His real aim was to abandon the last shred of the appearance of Negro representation in the Southern GOP. Negroes were thrown out of all leading posts in Southern state organizations and lily-white groups installed. Unable to do this with my father, he entered into a pact with Senator George of Georgia, who sponsored a bill to investigate corruption and bribery in the sale of federal patronage in the South. The bill was passed and George became chairman of the senate committee.

My father was the main target of the committee. The hearings took place in the federal building and lasted about ten days. My father was kept on the stand for a week. The press carried lurid stories of corruption and bribery that had been funneled through my father, of post offices being sold, of a Negro "humiliating" white men and women who had to come to him for jobs. What was the South—the sovereign state of Georgia—coming to? "Negro domination," shouted the press. And the terror and violence began again.

Actually nothing of a criminal or prosecutable nature was proved against my father. He was playing the game as astutely as his traducers; they knew that nothing could be proven. It was their aim to force my father out as national committeeman. In fact, Hoover had asked my father to resign and turn over the post to a white man—or the investigation would result. He refused to resign, knowing that the hatchet held over his head was intended for Negroes in the GOP organizations all over the South. It was a frame-up, and he chose to fight it—neither the first nor the last white supremacy legal frame-up against him.

But he eventually lost this round—from treachery within as well as the assaults from without—and he was forced out of his post. Hoover told my father—after calling him to Washington—that the unfavorable publicity which the Georgia organization had received made it necessary to change the whole leadership including my father.

I told him he should be bitter not only against Hoover but against the whole Republican Party. The party was bigger than Hoover, he replied. Moreover he had no other party to turn to—a plausible argument against which, at that time, I had no ready answer. The situation seemed to me a political dead-end.

Hoover, of course, was defeated by Roosevelt, and Hoover's dream of breaking the solid South went up in smoke. Since the Southern GOP organizations had no other source of existence than federal patronage, they wilted, becoming mere skeletons manned by the faithful who patiently looked forward to the day when the Republicans would win a presidential election. Twenty years is a long time to wait. . . .

For my father it was as if he were starting all over again. He was chairman of the Young Men's Republican Club of Georgia—most of the older stalwarts had long since died. He began to concentrate more and more on local politics, leading a vigorous campaign for the Negro population to vote. This was possible in city elections, if the poll-tax assessment was paid (the Negro was barred in state and national elections). Father waged a two-fold campaign: against the barriers in state and national elections, and among Negroes to kindle in them a sense of their power in city elections—even though they had to pay a poll tax. He soon realized, however, that the accumulation of unpaid poll taxes for the Negro as well as the white was so high that thousands were kept from voting.

My father had devoted his adult life to the Negro's realization of first-class citizenship. This had been his aim in all three of his major endeavors—the Odd Fellows, the Atlanta *Independent* and Republican politics. He had worked sincerely, ably, often brilliantly, to reform the ills of the existing semi-feudal plantation system. He never challenged the system itself and would have defied anyone who did. Within the reformist limitations of his thinking and activities, he made many contributions. His approach to the struggle for Negro liberation was conditioned by the material, social and economic forces which confronted him and which were dominant most of his life.

Notwithstanding his ability and achievements, his devotion and courage, he was regarded by the powers-that-be as "just another Georgia nigger." "Smart," maybe, as the tobacco-chewing Klansman had said at Covington, but just the same, a "nigger." When he got on a trolley car, he sat in the jim-crow section. He and his family lived in a ghetto. He was victimized by the Klan— in danger of being lynched and narrowly escaping it more than once. He was called "nigger" in the courts. He wore a "badge of inferiority" on his dark face, like other Negroes did. He had no rights a white man was bound to respect. He was fit only to be shot at and stoned when he moved too close to the iron curtain that separates Negroes from their manhood rights. While he took bold chances in challenging aspects of the jim-crow system, he did not challenge the basic source of the system or the system itself. No one knew better than he that there was a line drawn by the segregationists that he could not cross, and though he played dangerously close to it, he did not cross it. "I have to live here," he often said, taking a stand which could not be gainsaid.

Long before I had become aware of the labor and Communist movements, I had come to the conclusion that father's way was getting nowhere. I was attending Amherst and later Harvard, and I knew that I would return to be a "Georgia nigger." That, I was not going to be. My father had demonstrated the futility of Negro reformism—in that the success of individual Negroes did not raise the status of the Negro people, nor did it compensate for the brutal repression of the Negro masses. What it did too often was to degrade the individual successful Negro, making him a tool to obstruct the militant action of his own people. He could afford to say, "I've got to live here," in exchange for a crumb or two, an automobile, a better house, a middle-class standard of living which, even with a Negro leader's label on him, made his life a bit more bearable. And there were so few of these "successful" men.

For the Negro who had nothing whatsoever, it was difficult for me to see how he had anything to gain by making peace with the oppressor, and it was the Negro who had nothing who was the common denominator. But I had arrived at no alternative. During my high school days at Morehouse I had already begun to question my father's "way of struggle," so to speak. During my later schooling and afterwards, this developed into long and sometimes sharp ideological battles between us. My father, well intrenched as he was as a successful Negro leader, was too powerful for me, a stripling. So I conducted guerrilla warfare, often challenging the views he expressed in the *Independent*. I used to twit him about using his parental authority instead of sound arguments when he called me "impudent." This would make him furious. It was easy to foresee that we would part—the ideological gulf between us was too great. He was stubborn, and so was I. But the weak spot in my armor was that I had no alternative to offer. I knew only that his way had been found wanting. From my first critical feelings about his approach, I had been seeking, sometimes consciously and sometimes unconsciously, for another way. As I grew older, my search became more conscious. By the time I reached college and law school, the accumulation of experience as a Negro added fuel to this search, and it had become the consuming force of my life—with my studies taking a subordinate place in my mind.

Little by little, the relation between my father and me took on the character of an armed truce. It was more "armed" than "truce" when I abandoned the practice of law in 1936 and entered full time into the labor and Communist movements. And it broke out into open warfare in 1940, when the position of the Communists came into head-on clash with both major parties. I crossed swords with many of the Negro Republican spokesmen for the GOP, including my father. Sometimes father dismissed me as being merely a misguided upstart "tackling his daddy who was in politics before he was born."

Republicans suffered another severe beating at the hands of the Roosevelt New Deal coalition in 1944 before my father began to bend a little and question the political status quo. But he never broke.

For several years prior to his death, our personal relations had grown warm and close, in addition to being somewhat more mutually respectful. This was due principally to the fact that developments in the world had impressed him. He had told me earlier—and this was one of his more generous comments—"Son, you're wasting your time and your education on a lot of highfalutin' trash. It will be centuries before communist ideas get anywhere." Later he modified this considerably. He would say now and then, "Well, son, maybe I was wrong, perhaps your day is not so far away." When I was elected to the city council, he conceded at last that I had a right to my "radical, highfalutin' trash." And, as I have related, he enjoyed dangling this as a threat over the heads of the credentials committee at the Republican national convention in Chicago, in 1944.

My father was a product of his times; he reached his peak before there was any conscious Negro proletariat. Within the limitations of his period, he made a definite mark. From him I learned a deep and abiding respect for the common man and an equally deep antipathy for pomp and circumstance, for the hypocrisy and greed of the owning class. He liked to move among the people and had not the slightest use for exclusiveness of any sort. His Negro enemies were always among the Negro "elite," not among the masses. In an entirely different period, I was truly his son in this respect.

If our relationship was at times painful, I cannot say that it was on a personal basis—there were more basic reasons. It seems to me that it was a matter of older ideas giving place to new that was reflected in our relation, the conflict between two historical periods that neither he nor I fully understood at the time. There is always pain when the old is giving birth to the new.

He left me a personal heritage of sincerity, determination, courage and love of the common people. This was the kind of guidance in which the formative years of my life took shape. As a Lincoln Republican my father had a dream of realizing full manhood status for the Negro—in the broadest sense, I, as a Communist, am continuing his fight.

CHAPTER NINE

CIVIL RIGHTS IN THE POSTWAR PERIOD

Toward the end of World War II, the pro-fascist, Negro-hating forces which had been held in check during the war, began to break loose. Their purpose was to return the country to business-as-usual, to dissipate the illusions among certain sections of the people that the war against Hitler meant freedom, equality, democracy and peace at home.

The first section of the population to feel the rigors of reaction was, of course, the Negro people. They were forcibly reminded that regardless of what had happened to Hitler, Mussolini and Tojo, whatever had been said in the Atlantic Charter or at Teheran, Yalta and Cairo—and regardless of how many war heroes like Dorie Miller there had been—the Negro was still the victim of a system of national oppression and segregation. American imperialism had not changed its spots.

A shocking example of this occurred in the summer of 1946, when a mass lynching of Negroes took place near Monroe, Georgia, a small town about 40 miles north of Atlanta. Here, two veterans of World War II were seized by a Klan mob and brutally lynched; and then their wives, who had witnessed the lynching and could have identified the murderers, were also lynched. One of the most barbarous, cold-blooded crimes ever committed, it shocked the sensibilities of even the most callous and prejudiced.

The country was aroused as never before; the most conservative newspapers and radio chains were impelled by public sentiment to condemn this outrage. The Negro people all over the country were seething with anger.

In Harlem, we reacted at once. We organized a protest meeting

as quickly as possible—under the auspices of a committee organized to protest the lynching. Trade unions, professionals, ministers participated. More than two thousand heard the prayers
and brief addresses. It was a solemn gathering with few dry eyes
in the audience. Resolutions called for apprehension of the
lynchers, restitution to the families of the victims and the passage
of an anti-lynching bill. In the city council, I had introduced a
resolution memorializing the President and the FBI to take all
necessary steps. It was passed—but not without the councilmen
claiming I was making "political capital" of the lynching. We
tried to get action from Governor Dewey, with no success. Again,
my councilmanic office became a clearing house for the nation-
wide actions and protests. But nothing happened. The lynchers
went scot-free. Monroe, Georgia, became a virtual concentration
camp. A friend who investigated the scene said law and order had
broken down, that the Klan had taken complete control—
threatening and terrorizing anyone who opened his mouth.
And the lynchers were generally known.

The FBI issued its usual whitewash; it was, of course, "investigating to see if any federal law had been violated." Four American citizens, two of them World War II veterans, had been foully
murdered; local and state officials had refused to act, the Constitution had been trampled upon—and the FBI was investigating.
The lynchers could have had no greater encouragement than
J. Edgar Hoover's criminal failure of duty. No indictment, no
prosecution. The war against Hitler was won in Berlin but lost
in Monroe, Georgia.

That this attitude toward the lynchers encouraged the Ku
Kluxers was not long in being confirmed—lynchings broke out
all over the South and parts of the North. In Tennessee a mob
tried to shoot up the Negro section of a small city, but they got
more than they bargained for. A Negro veteran's eyes were
gouged out in South Carolina. During 1945 alone, a score or
more of completely unpunished lynchings took place.

In addition, Negroes were being kicked out of their war jobs.
In most of the South a premium was placed upon the head of any

Negro who was rash enough to try to vote. Bilbo and Rankin were in full control; on Southern plantations the battered bodies of Negro sharecroppers were found. The South was in the grip of a reign of terror directed primarily against the returning Negro veterans, whom the Klan-ridden, poll-tax regimes feared were most deeply infected with the expectation of freedom. They had to be intimidated; any grass-roots movement among the Negroes and their white supporters to realize the fruits of the war against Hitlerism had to be crushed.

The two major political parties were silent; they set up no committees to ferret out fascists, lynchers, anti-Semites, Ku-Klux-Klanners. Truman invoked no special session of congress upon this reign of terror—as he did to break the railroad strike. Things were getting back to normal—reaction was mobilizing again for the right war—against labor, the Negroes, the people at home; and against the socialist, colonial and anti-fascist movements abroad. The Communists and other progressives, having been among the foremost fighters against Hitler, were now to be the new victims of the monopolists' wrath. New scapegoats had to be manufactured. Amidst the spreading terror against Negroes there developed an economic crisis. The munitions manufacturers and the defense billionaires were facing huge cutbacks; they feared the loss of their fabulous profits coined out of World War II. The vast American productive machine, which had been expanded to supply the allies, was about to find its markets reduced substantially because of the depressed economic conditions in Britain, France and Italy, the shattering of the German and Japanese economies and, of course, the emergence of people's democracies in Eastern Europe. White supremacy, national chauvinism and religious persecution became important instruments in the hands of big business against the working class, in the face of the gathering economic recession. Negroes were the first and most persecuted victims.

The Negro people and their white supporters began to fight back. Negro leaders began to speak out; resistance by the masses became widespread; there was a nation-wide demand for action in

Washington. The Negro people were moving toward unity, and the Communists worked for concerted civil rights action that transcended race, color, creed or political view.

One day late in 1945 I sought an interview with Congressman Adam Clayton Powell to discuss how efforts could be pooled. He was quite concerned about the reactionary offensive against the Negro and his civil rights. We had a long and fruitful discussion and agreed to start the ball rolling nationally. We made plans to tackle the issue on the legislative front, singling out for attention: (1) the passage of anti-lynch and anti-poll-tax bills; (2) the enactment of an FEPC; (3) the ousting of Bilbo from the Senate—as well as other issues, such as the apprehension and death of the lynchers, defense of the Negro and other minorities from discrimination and persecution, enforcement of the 13th, 14th and 15th Amendments. We proposed to put this program before the opening session of Congress in the most dramatic manner by using methods in which the Negro masses could exert their initiative and participate.

We promptly issued a call for a national march to Washington to lay our program before the congress, the senate, the department of justice—and all other appropriate departments and leaders. The response from all over the country was overwhelming, and although we made no elaborate physical preparations, when the day arrived, approximately 600 delegates from more than 30 states arrived and converged on the capitol.

Here we sent a delegation to the congressional authorities and got permission to use an assembly hall in the House Office Building; a steering committee was elected; the delegates were organized into groups to see key congressmen and senators. Some were dispatched to the attorney general, to Hoover's office, to the President's assistant and other government officials. Our demand was that the FEPC be brought up in the senate immediately, and that anti-lynch and anti-poll-tax legislation be enacted. The delegation saw Senator Wayne Morse and received a promise he would take the lead for the FEPC in the Senate. He did, but most ineffectively, holding that "nothing would be done now."

The delegates made a vivid impression, and the experience

gained by them was priceless; many learned for the first time the callousness, ignorance and hyprocrisy that characterized some of the legislators. In an effort to relieve themselves of responsibility, the Democrats brought up the FEPC under conditions where a defeat was certain, because of the reactionary cloture rule. Passage of an FEPC bill had been a plank in both platforms in 1944. The delegates had seen directly that this was a subterfuge to get the Negro and civil rights vote.

This delegation was only the first; the continuing reign of terror had exacted a toll of more than 40 lynchings by the summer of 1946. The rosy promises given to our delegation in January had proved to be a mirage. Another delegation consisting of several thousand—"the Crusade against Lynching"—was organized. It was my privilege to be associated with the Crusade and to participate in it. There were many outstanding Negro and white leaders among the sponsors; the thousands who attended came from almost every conceivable type of organization —on a strictly nonpartisan, nonsectarian basis. They were disciplined, dignified and mobile, although far too large for any one assembly point. And by that time the situation had grown much worse, the lines of battle sharper. We could not secure a government building, but officials did see delegations. Again the issues raised covered the range of civil rights questions and stressed the shocking increase in lynching.

All in all, the Crusade was extremely impressive and worthwhile. It received national prominence and attention, the reactionary press and radio, of course, calling it a "Communist-inspired invasion of the capital." Along with the earlier demonstration called by Representative Powell and myself, it helped to focus national—and even international—attention upon the lynch terror and the struggles of the people against it. Congressmen and senators became sensitive about such delegations and were compelled to take note of them—if only negatively. But the demonstrations were hitting home. While the Washington bureaucrats fiddled, the people were becoming more and more militant and united.

Reactionary politicians began to crack down. As the pressure got tougher, they refused to see the people, but neither the Negroes nor their constantly augmented white allies were discouraged. The civil rights and anti-lynch issues were the focal point of the entire liberation movement.

One of the new features of the recent period, beginning with Roosevelt's New Deal, is the admission by the ruling class and the government of widespread discrimination against the Negro and other minorities. There was Roosevelt's report on economic conditions in the South and, lately, the Truman Civil Rights Report, together with documentary material on discrimination in the nation's capital—where even the dog of a Negro is not permitted to be buried in the same cemetery with that of a white person. Similar reports by official and semi-governmental bodies in all parts of the country have made often startling disclosures on the mistreatment of the Negro and other ethnic groups.

It took many years for the ruling class thus to take official notice of discrimination against the Negro people. When it finally did so, it was only because of the incessant pounding of the Negro people themselves and of their working class and progressive allies, including those god-awful Communists. But nothing has been done about these abominable conditions. The data in President Truman's Civil Rights Report was useful in exposing the monstrous oppression of the Negro, but this was entirely incidental to the purposes for which this report was made public, namely, to ensnare votes for the corrupt Democratic Party machine. Usually, the publication of such official reports serve the cheapest demagogic purposes: to enable reactionary Democratic and Republican politicians to sweeten the stench of racial oppression with the perfume of liberal phrases and hypocritical promises.

If investigations and statistical studies would produce freedom, the Negro people would be living in a utopia. Truth is, the Negro has been investigated to death. But the Negro people today are wise to the run-around that occurs when a public official "meets" a complaint of jim-crow by appointing a commission "to study the question."

In any case, the investigations and statistics do confirm that the Negro is the most oppressed section of the American people, although not the only oppressed section. Further, they show that the oppression of the Negro is systematic and organized—that it is both part of and the result of a system that is national both in scope and character. This much, it seems to me, is clear to even the most prejudiced observer.

The rub comes when one attempts to take these conclusions further. The oppression of the Negro is not accidental, nor is it the result of some malfunctioning of the capitalist system. On the contrary, it is deliberate on the part of the monopoly capitalists who derive super-profits from the oppression of the Negro. The national oppression of the Negro is due not to capitalism failing to work properly but to capitalism working as properly and perfectly as it can. The capitalists and even their most liberal apologists avoid this conclusion like the devil does holy water.

It is precisely this system that must be faced up to if one is to deal radically and basically with the brutal oppression of the Negro. Otherwise, one is tilting with windmills. To divert people away from this central question, in their various reports the capitalists may "cry out in pain," but it is the Negro who takes the blows. It has been well said that the capitalist will do anything for the Negro but get off his back. In fact, the capitalist is devising constantly new ways and subterfuges for staying on the Negro's back and everything he does has this aim. Any view to the contrary is either pure illusion or willful deceit, and the marketplace of ideas is already glutted with damaged goods of this stripe.

I would like to follow the conclusions from the statistics all the way. I approach the subject not primarily from the angle that Negroes live in so many units of tuberculosis-ridden slums in this or that community, but from the angle of the man-made system that brings these slums about and of what can be done to banish them here now, and tomorrow, everywhere. I am mainly concerned here with direction and long-range objectives more than with transient developments, although the two are intimately connected. . . .

In my youth, as I have written previously, I was deeply impressed with the ability and potentials of the Negro community. Years later, when I was introduced to the Communist advocacy of self-determination for the Negro majorities in the South, it fitted my experience. I knew of the Negro's capacity for self-government and that he needed a form of self-determination to attain political freedom and economic equality to which he was entitled by his dignity and genius. Such a program, it seemed to me, could free him from the stunted status assigned him by American capitalism and could unleash the creative capacities that would enrich the country and the world. I knew of no other program that offered such dignity and basic equality to the Negro people.

In the Communist science, I learned that socialism alone could give the Negro his full freedom, for only under socialism could he enjoy full self-determination. Thus I became an advocate of socialism, believing that the working class would in time provide the revolutionary leadership needed to attain socialism.

CHAPTER TEN

MY FRIEND PETE CACCHIONE DIES

On November 27, 1946, one of the biggest and warmest of human hearts ceased to beat. Peter V. Cacchione—"Pete," as we affectionately knew him—a member of the New York city council from Brooklyn and an outstanding Communist leader—suffered a heart attack and passed away. We had left each other scarcely two hours before, after a brief meeting of the city council. He was smiling and in good spirits, as he invariably was, despite the handicap of a serious illness which had almost totally impaired his vision.

As Pete's closest co-worker for the last years of his life, I was deeply shocked. His death was a great personal loss—the greatest I had ever sustained in the death of a friend. The triumphs and defeats we had tasted in the city council for those four years, the abuse and the struggles we had shared, the redbaiting we had to endure, all had welded us into the strongest kind of personal friendship, based upon our common convictions and our common struggles to uphold them. Pete's death affected me deeply for a long time afterward.

He was, in a sense, a casualty of the class struggle. He had fallen in battle, after being shaken and wounded many times by poverty, heartbreaks, physical privation and police brutality. His life had never been easy. And he was a fighter. His death was a tremendous loss to the cause of freedom and peace and to our party. Messages of condolence came not alone from the workers and the democratic groups in New York whom he served directly, but from Maine to California and from Europe and Asia.

At his funeral, not only trade unions and people's organizations but also public officials—especially Republican and Democratic councilmen—paid tribute to him. The latter feared to offend the working masses of Brooklyn, who had shown their

love and respect by three times electing him to the city council—
the last time with the highest vote in the borough. My having to
preside so occupied me that I had no time to heed my deep grief.
Mayor O'Dwyer, who had a prudent respect for Pete's stature
among the voters of Brooklyn, issued a perfunctory statement of
regret.

The hypocritical tributes of the bourgeois politicians were
belied by the fact that just three weeks prior to Pete's death, proportional representation had been defeated by the Tammany-
Republican machines under the slogan: "Kick Cacchione and
Davis out of the city council." During that campaign, we were
called every conceivable name, and Pete had spent mountains of
energy campaigning in Brooklyn. It was said that we were "subversive," that we were "allied with Satan," that we were traitors,
that we were seeking to undermine the city government and that
we were agents of a foreign power with a barbaric political philosophy. The only way to keep us out of the council was to defeat
PR. None had been more hysterical than some of the very councilmen who now shed crocodile tears at Pete's funeral. The councilmen who did not attend the funeral or speak had joined in
the unanimous resolution of the city council eulogizing Pete's
membership.

But even in the city council, where eulogies for deceased members were routine, there was haggling over the resolution to be
adopted on his death. The resolution was delayed because they
took so long to agree on whether he was a "good councilman"
or "a good American." The latter they flatly refused to say, even
though he had given his life in the cause of democracy and good
government; had built an outstanding progressive council record,
had been a World War I veteran and had sold more World War
II bonds than all the Tammany councilmen put together. When
other council members died, they painted them in such glowing
terms that one would have thought they were talking about
Thomas Jefferson and Abraham Lincoln rolled into one. Although it was customary to give the family of the deceased member an engraved and embossed copy of the resolution, with the
city seal affixed, signed by every councilman, this was not done.

Nor could they be honest even about this small courtesy. They procrastinated, hemmed and hawed and gave Mrs. Cacchione so many transparent excuses that it became embarrassing to mention it. Feeling by now that the anguish of the people had died down, they sobered up and returned to anti-Communist business as usual.

Pete Cacchione's contributions to the people of New York were legion. His initial election in 1941 was the first breakaway of any considerable segment of New York voters from the two-party system—and constituted a break on the highest political level thus far. Never before had any one been elected whose party stood for socialism and who campaigned on the defeat of the two-party system. His election gave heart and courage to the independent voters all over the city and nation. Utilizing the relatively democratic electoral weapon of proportional representation, he had cut through the two-party monopoly, which became progressively weaker during succeeding elections—until Tammany had a majority of one in the council after the last PR election in 1945, and was compelled to collaborate with the Republicans or the Liberal Party in order to steamroller a two-thirds majority measure through the council.

And Pete had contributed to this situation by running as a Communist, meeting the redbaiters head-on and leaving no doubt that he had been freely chosen by the electorate. It was his bold snatching of victory from the stranglehold of reaction in 1941 that prepared the way for my election in 1943.

In many respects, the political and ideological conditions which faced him were more difficult than those which faced me. At the time I ran, the country had for two years been engaged in the war against the fascist axis, the Soviet-American alliance was well developed, and a high degree of national unity existed behind the war effort. Such an atmosphere made it more difficult for the fascists and redbaiters, and less difficult for the democratic and anti-fascist forces.

When Pete ran in 1941, however, America had not entered the war and the reactionaries were still effective and powerful. A great debate was taking place as to whether America should enter the world struggle against fascism, although it was clear that the national interest of the country dictated her participation. Stupid and venal political leaders were hoping that the hatred of Hitler Germany could be turned into the desired imperialist assault against the Soviet Union. But forces more powerful than the trusts and the reactionaries won the day, and the determination of the American people to defend the independence of their country won out over the hatred of the Trumans for the Soviet Union and communism.

It was amidst this ideological confusion that Pete's campaign had to be waged. As the head of the party in Brooklyn, he helped arm the organization with the policies necessary to defeat the arguments of the redbaiting Democrats and Republicans.

His role in the council was unique. Elected three times, he had only one piece of legislation passed—a resolution against the removal of price controls, which would have threatened the living standards of the working people. But no member ever introduced so much progressive legislation that was later appropriated by the Democratic majority and enacted into law, or watered down and passed over the name of some Tammany wardheeler. On the other hand, many a reactionary piece of legislation never saw the light of day because of Pete's fiery and capable opposition. Sometimes he was joined by other liberals but often he was alone. His dynamic presence in council was a sharp reminder to the majority that under proportional representation the voters could replace any councilman who rode roughshod over their interests. Pete's presence and his responsible attitude sobered them up.

The biggest single contribution Pete made was his fight for the five-cent fare. His name tops the list of individuals who sought to prevent this piece of highway robbery by the bankers and real estate interests. The vanguard role of our party, the initiative of labor, and the united front of consumers and low-income groups were combined under his leadership. Pete's tireless energy, his painstaking accumulation of data and statistics, his damaging blows against venal politicians, his formidable zest for the fight turned the ten-cent-fare crowd upside down.

The city council was not the only arena of struggle; Pete journeyed to Albany, led delegations of workers to lobby among the assemblymen and state senators. Many shifted their position —or at least pretended to—under the pressure of the facts marshalled by Pete and his co-workers.

And it must be remembered that in addition to being an outstanding public official, Peter Cacchione was a staunch leader of our party. In his practical work and accumulated political acumen, he demonstrated that we were in a new stage of parliamentary struggle in which important sections of the working class were sufficiently advanced to elect representatives of the party of socialism as public officials. It was Pete who helped to shape state and national campaigns, transmitting the vibrant understanding and skill he had gained in his own experience in this field of activity.

Upon his election as the first Communist to hold public office in the United States, Pete richly confirmed the fact that party leadership was not incompatible with mass leadership. He helped to make the decisions of the party and then he tested them in his work among the masses. Beloved and respected in the party, the position he took during the 1945 internal crisis helped to consolidate the membership against the bourgeois capitulations of Browderism.

Few knew of the physical handicaps under which he suffered during the latter years of his life, the greatest of which was his impaired vision. He had about one-tenth of normal eyesight; he could scarcely make out large images five yards ahead of him. He could not read at all and could sign his name only when someone guided his hand. The party put at his disposal one of its most reliable members, who served as his eyes, reading all important publications and data to him—beginning with the *Daily Worker*. And during the last three years of his life Pete also developed a very serious chronic heart ailment.

Completely mastering the potentially depressing effect of his near-blindness, he asked no quarter, shrugging off even the most well-meaning attempt to treat him as handicapped. Yet some of us knew—I, above all, because of my constant work with him—

that nothing gnawed more at his vitals than the handicap of his blindness in his work in the council. He was one of the best informed members of the council; he knew the city of New York as he knew his own name—its population, its vital statistics, its business composition and industries, its slums, the area of its boroughs, and the like. He knew the financial setup of the city, its debts and assets, while his phenomenal knowledge of all aspects of the transportation system was very irksome to the propertied advocates of the ten-cent fare. It was not very often that the Tammany gentry could get away with any humbuggery about New York with Pete around. On one occasion he took the floor and detailed the vital statistics of the city with his uncanny accuracy—the number of births and deaths and marriages, the number of children born during the preceding few years, the mortality rates, and so on. Afterwards, other councilmen often consulted him before hazarding a correction from him in the debate.

Sometimes his near-blindness was the occasion for an unfortunate incident. Once he got up to take the floor after one of the members of the council had finished. But another member of the council had preceded Pete in asking for the floor and the president of the council had properly recognized him ahead of Pete. Pete, however, had not seen this happen and began speaking at the same time. Whereupon the other councilman started berating Pete, assailing him as "rude and disruptive, violating the rules of the council in a manner typical of Communists." Bursting with rage, I leapt to my feet to denounce the thoughtless fellow and to inform him that Pete was not able to see that he had been recognized first. I demanded an apology to Pete from the insulting redbaiter and was going to lash him further, but the president intervened, taking the blame upon himself for not stating audibly the name of the man he had recognized. And Pete, usually far quicker of temper than I, was as cool as a cucumber. Sitting by my side, he grabbed me by the coattail, pulled me to my seat and said in a quiet voice, "Ben, don't carry it further. I don't want an issue made of my eyesight. After all, I was wrong." I understood, and immediately deferred to his wishes.

On the council floor, I was Pete's eyes. I read him the legislative calendar, the bills up for consideration, preparing my own remarks in memorandum form so that they could be relayed to him. There was a division of labor, so to speak, between us, Pete handling all matters of finance except the city budget—a ponderous document of small print and figures which tired even my eyes—and I handling those matters that affected civil rights and preparing all draft data on such questions. Together Pete and I handled labor and trade union questions.

Only once did he and I have a sharp difference of opinion during a council meeting, but that was entirely between ourselves and did not reach the council floor. Once Councilman Roger, a crackpot Republican who hardly knew the time of day, launched a silly and revolting attack upon the Negro people. The incident arose in the course of the passage of my annual resolution memorializing Negro History Week as an official observance of the city. For reasons of their own, the councilmen almost invariably passed the resolution unanimously. This time, however, Councilman Roger took the floor to point out that "we should stop petting the Negroes and playing up to them by passing such a resolution . . . after all, if they were like other minority groups, they would be in control of things instead of being the underdogs . . . if they weren't, something must be wrong with them," *ad nauseam*. I was on my feet instantly, but Pete pulled me down. Meanwhile, someone else got the floor—while Pete and I were arguing about who should answer Roger. It was a bitter argument, but I finally gave in to Pete, who insisted that although it was only natural that I should want to defend my own people, my strong feelings could not be the decisive factor. He pointed out that a Marxist understands that it is the duty of the white worker to rise to the defense of the Negro people when they are under attack from white supremacists, and that it was a political question, with the obligation of initiative resting on him first. He was correct, and I yielded reluctantly, for I hated to lose this priceless opportunity to get at Roger, who was constantly berating the Communists.

Pete took the floor and gave Roger two blows for one. But he did more. He traced the development of the Negro people in the

United States from the time the first African slaves were landed in Jamestown, in 1620, to the present day. And he did it so impressively, with such an enviable command of the various periods of the Negro's struggle for freedom, with such a comprehensive command of the contributions and the sufferings of the Negro people that he held the entire council spellbound. Pete's defense of Negro History Week was a work of art, but the council was so enthralled by Pete's eloquent rejoinder to Roger that it did not notice that he had occupied the floor for a full half-hour, instead of the usually allotted ten minutes. Debate was closed, and the resolution was passed almost unanimously. That day's session belonged to Pete.

His speech impressed me deeply, although I had heard him speak effectively on almost every kind of occasion. I told him as much, and of the pride the Negro people would have felt in hearing their history and contributions so ably expounded by a white worker. He beamed. We had a sort of silent agreement about evaluating each other's floor debates. Perhaps it leaned a bit in the direction of a "mutual admiration society." But we were so frequently and so bitterly denounced by the Tammanyites that we hardly needed to berate each other. We took great pains to commend each other on "an exceptionally good job." When we fell below par, we would say nothing in the Council. But a few days later, when both of us had had time to think, we would dissect an unsatisfactory performance from every angle and determine how we could do better on the subject next time.

Pete had gone no further than the eighth grade in school, but he often put to shame professors with multiple degrees whose only answer to his dialectical wisdom was to say, "Who listens to Communists?" Born of poor Italian-American parents in up-state New York, he had been a railroad worker like his father. The Italian immigrants who had helped build the railroads in the Northeast were brutally exploited for the benefit of the first giant American fortunes. They were among the "cheap foreign labor" that the Vanderbilts, Goulds and Morgans imported from Europe for super-exploitation and fabulous profits—just as the Negro slaves had been taken from Africa to provide "cheap labor."

Pete had felt every injustice upon his own back. He had known poverty, hunger and brutality as an unemployed worker and veteran during the Hoover depression days. His first knowledge of New York was as a despised, disinherited occupant of a Bowery flophouse by night and a frequenter of soup kitchens by day. When, in the early 30's, he became a member of the unemployed veterans' organization, he soon revealed his militant qualities as a leader of the Bonus March to Washington, where he and thousands of other World War I veterans and their families were tear-gassed by General MacArthur, on the orders of President Hoover. When he led a workers' demonstration to Albany to seek state unemployment aid, the demonstration was ambushed and savagely attacked by the police and Pete was badly and painfully mauled. There are none who understand suffering like those who have suffered themselves.

Widespread discrimination existed and still exists against Italians and other foreign-born minorities even in "liberal" New York, and Pete was peculiarly sensitive to the oppression of minorities—particularly the Negro people. He had the gift of communicating this understanding to Negroes—not alone by his Communist activities but by his daily personal attitude toward them and their organizations. In repeated elections, the Negro community of Bedford-Stuyvesant was among his most enthusiastic supporters. When he went to the Negro community at the time he was trying to break the two-party stranglehold that prevented the election of a Negro councilman from Brooklyn, he urged them to vote first for the Negro candidate and only after they did that to vote for him.

During Pete's first term in the city council, some of the diehard members didn't speak to him for the entire two years. But Pete shrugged it off with a quip. He had a mischievous, infectious sense of humor. When, upon his first election in 1941, he was called upon to make a speech to about 3,000 tally clerks, officials, defeated candidates and campaign workers, everyone expected an extended and weighty address analyzing the world situation in classic Marxist fashion, or delineating his council plans. Pete took the microphone and said: "I'm just a plain old Brooklynite who's looking forward to the Brooklyn Dodgers winning the pennant next year." Then he sat down.

He knew how to squelch a heckler with a seemingly innocent non-political remark. One instance of this occurred on the occasion when, as a newly elected councilman, he was to join the others in visiting the outgoing council. The new councilmen would be given the privileges of the floor—which meant that the council president assigned two members to escort each guest to the rostrum to be introduced.

All sorts of wild stories had been appearing to the effect that Pete would not be seated because he was a Communist. (The New York State legislature had gotten away with a trick like that against five Socialists elected to the assembly 20 years earlier.) When Pete went on this first visit to the council, he was pointedly denied the privileges of the floor. The reporters gathered around him immediately afterwards, needling him for a statement and actually spying on Pete to find out his plans and transmit them to the Tammanyites. One aggressive reporter said: "Mr. Cacchione, there is a concerted effort to prevent you from taking your seat. I don't mind telling you that a group of taxpayers are planning to file suit against you. . . . Surely, you're going to fight this. How do you feel about being denied the courtesy of the floor?"

Pete spoke almost casually: "When strangers came to our house, my mother taught me to be courteous to them. Evidently some mothers didn't teach their sons that way."

In any chronicle of my Communist development and activity, the name of Peter V. Cacchione could not possibly be omitted. Two comparatively short years with him in the council were an invaluable education to me—a source of Marxist guidance blended with warm human regard for my welfare. No concern of mine was too small to engage his attention and solicitude. But it was from Pete in action that I learned most, for he based all his work on a scrupulous marshalling of facts. He didn't care where these facts came from; he only asked: were they true? He was bold and fearless. The enthusiastic spirit characteristic of him pervaded the entire Brooklyn party organization which he led. Although he was attacked from many quarters for his doggedly held convictions, I do not believe that he had a single personal enemy.

Pete never forgot that he was a son of the working class. It accounted for his uncanny ability to divine the issues, yearnings and aspirations of his class. I was comforted and inspired because I knew that if Pete could today feel with the sensitivity of a seismograph the problems of the Negro people, millions of white American workers would do so tomorrow.

After the death of this man, who was something new in American electoral history and who was an anchor of personal and political strength to me, the remainder of my term in the council was not the same. But I pledged to redouble my efforts in behalf of the Negro people and all the democratic elements of our city. Remembering Pete, I was never satisfied with my performance.

CHAPTER ELEVEN

TRIAL AND SENTENCE

(Since there is no consecutive story of the Smith Act trial in the manuscript, the following passages were gathered together from various sections of the author's notes.)

This is where I came in.

Nineteen years ago, one hot sunny afternoon in June in Atlanta, I offered my legal services to a young Negro Communist who had been indicted for attempting to overthrow the government of the state of Georgia by force and violence. His so-called crime carried the death penalty. His actual offense was that he had led a demonstration of Negro and white workers to the county courthouse to demand relief and unemployment insurance—a perfectly legal and democratic action guaranteed by the U.S. Constitution. I had read the brief item buried away in the Atlanta Constitution and I became so outraged by the patent frame-up that I immediately went to visit him in jail.

Now *I* am in jail. For that visit set off a chain of events in my life which led to the Foley Square*conviction and the heavy sentences imposed on myself and ten other leaders of the Communist Party. Six months after that visit to Herndon, I joined the Communist Party. It required only a few moments to achieve that honor—as long as it took me to sign an application card. But my whole life as a son of an oppressed people had prepared me for that moment.

History repeats itself. The Smith Act, under which the Communist Party and its leaders were hounded and prosecuted, was but an updated version of the Georgia insurrection law under which Herndon was convicted. At least Herndon was charged

* Site of the Federal Courthouse in New York City.

with attempting to overthrow the government. The Smith Act stipulates that it is enough to "conspire" to "teach and advocate" the overthrow of the government by force and violence. On its face, the Smith Act is even more patently unconstitutional than the Georgia insurrection law.

In the Foley Square trial the government sank to the level of a cooked-up farce, rigged to fit the aggressive war policies of the monopolists. It is certainly not comforting to the ruling circles of the United States to realize that they cannot afford to permit the arguments of its opponents to be offered freely in the market-place but can only answer those arguments with the force and violence of jail.

A week after we were convicted we were brought from the federal detention house at West Street before Judge Medina for sentencing. The courtroom was packed. When our case was called, we were ordered to stand. Judge Medina asked if we had anything to say before we were sentenced. Eugene Dennis, general secretary of the Communist Party, and I spoke. Gene pointed out that the conviction was a blow to the cause of peace and liberty. I declared it was an attack upon the Negro people—their long struggle for freedom and first-class citizenship, and that the conviction was timed to assist my defeat as the chosen representative of the Negro people. When Dennis and I had finished, Judge Medina called each of our names and sentenced each of us to five years and $10,000 fine—with the exception of Bob Thompson, who got three years and $10,000 fine.

Originally, the maximum sentence for our offense was ten years. But during the period between the passage of the Smith Act and our conviction, congress reduced the maximum to five years—and Judge Medina had given us the maximum. One thought crowded everything else out of my mind—in the whole history of the United States, with more than 5,000 brutal and monstrous lynchings of Negroes, not one perpetrator had received a sentence of five months—to say nothing of five years.

As we wheeled around to take our seats again, I looked out into the audience and saw people weeping. It was a sad day for American democracy—the twilight of popular liberties.

There were some illusions that my case might have been different, my sentence less severe. This was based on the light sentences received by such public officials as Congressmen May and Parnell Thomas who were only thieves who had stolen from the people—in a class with robbers, thugs, racketeers, and the like. They were merely unlucky in being caught—otherwise they were corporals in the political army that the monopolists maintain in Washington and throughout the United States.

Henry Winston and I received the longest prison sentences for political opinions any Negroes had received in modern America. We were the first Negro victims of the Smith Act. And I was the first member of the New York city council ever to have been expelled from that body and, of course, the first Negro. It may well be that I was the first Negro ever to have been expelled from any legislative body in the history of the country—and certainly the first Communist to be so expelled. I also received the longest sentence of any elected public official in recent American history.

Actually, it was the purpose of the court in giving me the maximum sentence to intimidate and terrorize all militant Negroes, to serve notice that a fight for free and equal citizenship would be met with severe reprisals.

During the trial I was to discover that my entry into the practice of law 17 years earlier was but a part of a "retroactive conspiracy," further evidence of my "menacing and criminal" activities. During my cross-examination, the U.S. prosecutor trotted out a copy of my application to become a member of the bar in Georgia. Among other questions the applicant was required to answer there was one asking whether the applicant was a resident of the state of Georgia and whether he intended, in good faith, to practice law there. A few years after I opened my law office (approximately three or four years) I gave up the practice of law and moved my residence to New York.

The prosecutor attempted to prove that I had obtained admission to the bar by fraud, that I had never intended to practice law in Georgia, and that at the time I signed my application my residence was not in the state. This was the method used to impeach my credibility as a witness and defendant in the Foley Square trial. Furthermore, it was an open invitation to the state of Georgia to institute proceedings to disbar me, and to the Federal District Court of the Atlanta circuit to do likewise.

Thus my admission to the Georgia bar in 1932 became pertinent to the Smith Act—which was not enacted until 1940! It was necessary for the U.S. government to use one big lie to cover an even bigger one.

The three weeks we spent at West Street—which most assuredly is a jail—was no earnest of what we were to experience in the real-thing prisons. One might view West Street as a preface to the oppressive and monotonous period that followed. We all lived in the same "bullpen"—which does not happen in big-time prisons, where Negro and white inmates are segregated. We ate together and we saw movies together—which is also a departure from the segregation in federal prisons. There were Southern inmates and guards at West Street, but they did not seem to mind. In fact, I formed an acquaintance with a young white fellow from Kentucky, and his constant diatribes against segregation and discrimination—at the top of his voice—made me look like a parlor pink.

We were also permitted to see our friends and relatives daily, and were allowed private consultations with our attorneys whenever necessary. We talked, played dominoes, checkers, chess, cards, and visited other cells. We had the books we wished. Indeed within the limits of the straitjacket of confinement, the place was tolerable. Nevertheless, after ten days we were happy to get some routine-breaking assignments. Dennis was assigned to the hospital; Bob Thompson and Carl Winter became painters; John Gates handled big crates in the warehouse; Henry Winston and Gil Green were in the clothing issue departments, and Jack Stachel, a former needle-trades worker, was in clothing repair. John Williamson, with a bad back, and Irving Potash, also not strong, were idle. I became an administrative clerk checking prisoners in and out. Gus Hall was ultimately made the equivalent of head waiter in the dining room. He was very generous with the government's bread—which he turned into a socialized commodity among the prisoners.

Queer things happen in jail. While I was on check-in duty, in walked five arrested members of Amtorg, the Soviet Union's trading organization. None of them spoke English well enough to make themselves understood, and none of the West Street officials spoke Russian. The wheels of American justice came to a standstill. And I could not perform my duty of checking them in. I was glad to meet them, but I couldn't say "I'm glad to see you here."

The officials had to send out a call for anyone who could speak Russian. Finally they ended up with Potash. He translated the instructions of the guard, and my requests as to their names and their personal possessions. They didn't like any of this—and I could hardly blame them. Finally, I had Potash tell them that we were the convicted leaders of the Communist Party, so that they might at least know we were not part of that setup. But that didn't seem to allay their skepticism. Finally, one of them said, "You want us to believe you American Communists are running the capitalist prisons?"

The Russians gave the authorities a tussle—they would stay nowhere but in a cell all to themselves. They invoked diplomatic immunity; they refused to comply with the prison instructions until their consulate representative arrived. And they constantly dinned into the ears of the officials: "I guess this is more of your American justice." And right they were. For if they had been Franco representatives, instead of Soviet citizens, they would never have been subjected to such indignities.

Later, when they saw the newspapers, they recognized us, and when we met in the passageways, the tension had left their faces. But actually they were not chummy with anyone, evidently guarding well the dignity and interests of their homeland against the low tricks which the U.S. government had so many times visited not only against socialist countries but also against their own workers.

The three weeks at the Federal Detention House on West Street was the longest jail sentence I had ever served. The worst was yet to come. At this enforced avocation, I was to become a seasoned veteran.

When we were sentenced Judge Medina again denied us bail, pending appeal. We were returned to West Street. On the outside, bedlam broke loose, with demands from all strata of the American people that we be permitted bail. The clamor mounted, even from the Americans for Democratic Action, as well as from countless unions and middle-class and professional elements. The party did a heroic job. The Civil Rights Congress in less than ten days secured a bail fund of more than a million dollars from public subscription—a real tribute to the CRC and to the sturdy, democratic Americans, Negro and white, who contributed.

At West Street, we "elected not to serve" our sentences. This meant that we could not, under the law, be shipped out to prison until our appeals had been finally adjudicated in court. But we weren't sure, in view of how legal justice had fared, what was going to happen. We proved to be correct; three weeks from the day of our conviction and remanding to jail, we were freed on bail granted by the Circuit Court of Appeals. The circuit court, unlike the swashbuckling Medina, took pains to see that at least the formalities of constitutional procedure were observed in our cases. It overruled Medina, took the prosecutors to task for their crudeness; and now again illusions began to soar—like the stockmarket at its wildest—and just as false. For, six months later, when our cases came up for appeal on their merits, Judge Learned Hand, senior judge of the circuit—a jurist who, I had learned in law school, was a liberal—delivered himself of an opinion that upheld our conviction unanimously. Hand retired a few months later; his opinion in our case was the valedictory to his own liberal reputation.

I had been in prison only a few months when I learned that the U.S. Supreme Court had granted a hearing to our lawyers' appeal from the contempt sentences imposed upon them at the Foley Square trial by Judge Medina. This meant that the Supreme Court in less than five months had reversed itself. In June, when our convictions were upheld by the court, it had refused a hearing to our attorneys. In October, the court granted what they had refused. This, of course, had no legal effect on the case of the eleven, but it did affect the lawyers. Justices Black and Douglas had dissented in June; their dissents became majority opinions in October. What happened to the court in the interim? My opinion is that the court majority heard, if only faintly, the rumblings among the people during those four months. When it hears the rumblings more distinctly from American workers and others aroused about their peace and dwindling liberties, perhaps it would reverse itself where the eleven were concerned. The explanations of the court's opinions and changes of opinion are to be found much nearer to earth than to heaven.

CHAPTER TWELVE

LIFE IN THE TERRE HAUTE
PENITENTIARY

I arrived at the Terre Haute penitentiary July 10, 1951. (That the city of Terre Haute, birthplace of Eugene V. Debs, should be the site of a dungeon for working-class champions is enough to make the great socialist leader turn over in his grave.) On July 6, six of us—Dennis, Gates, Williamson, Winter, Potash and I—had been transported on the prison bus from the Federal Detention House on West Street to Lewisburg Penitentiary in Pennsylvania. The seventh prisoner, Stachel, remained in New York to be routed directly to the Danbury, Conn., federal penitentiary. At Lewisburg, we were divided and routed as follows: Dennis and Gates to Atlanta; Winter and Williamson to Lewisburg; Potash to Leavenworth; and I to Terre Haute. In October 1951, Gus Hall was kidnapped from Mexico in gangster fashion by the FBI and later sent to Leavenworth.

Because of his heart ailment, Stachel was sent to Danbury, supposedly one of the "easiest" prisons. (I shall never forget Prosecutor McGohey's reply to a humane and reasonable request for the continuance of Stachel's bail: "Oh, indeed, your honor, prison is good for heart ailments.")

As can be seen, the government took pains to divide us, allowing no more than two of the leaders in the same penitentiary. It is anybody's guess why, but it added to our punishment, denying us companionship and making the going that much harder for those who were alone. It denied us the opportunity to pool our mutual knowledge and interests. The government perhaps feared our being together even in jail, encircled by umpteen officers and steel bars every foot or so. But this hardly explains the special honor extended to me. I was stuck off by myself in a state notorious for its Ku Klux Klan and so close to the site of the Cicero, Illinois, white-supremacy outbreak, I could almost feel it down my neck. Since I was the only Negro among the jailed Communist leaders, a terrific problem confronted the champions of democracy who run the government. To have put me together with a white leader would have placed too great a strain upon the system of segregation prevailing in the federal prison system. The friendship which would have been demonstrated between me and one of my fellow-Communists would have been a bad example for the other Negro and white prisoners.

Actually this was my first time in jail—except for a hot moment for union picketing and the three-week stretch in West Street. In prisoner's parlance, a five-year sentence is not regarded as exactly beginner's luck. By and large, I have been treated like all the other Negro prisoners. The occasional exceptions did not mean special favors—which I neither asked for nor received. Although I am without experience in this field, prison is prison and the life becomes almost insufferable at times. The atmosphere is oppressive and the prison routine enervating. Washington, in violation of even the prison rules, clamped extra restrictions upon my correspondence, allowing me at first to correspond with no one but my sister and my attorney. Inmates are normally permitted to have seven on their correspondents' list.

In prison, one is beset by mental frustration, emotional and spiritual starvation and by a benumbing prison routine enforced by the threat of violence in the prison's punitive measures. Both extremes are to be found—the bitterest cursing and the most disgusting cringing—sometimes both in the same prisoner. There are all sorts of complex cross-currents which one does well to be aware of.

One learns soon to guard against three major hazards—deterioration of health, mental stagnation, emotional imbalance. It is particularly depressing to become ill in prison. To prevent this, you can take exercise in the "recreation yard"—baseball, softball, basketball, football, calisthenics, weight-lifting, horseshoe pitching and other sports. In my zeal for exercise, soon after

I arrived I sprained my ankle playing baseball. Then, as luck would have it, I had trouble with a displaced disc in my back and ended up in the prison hospital for three weeks. As a result, I had to sleep on a bedboard in my cell—not that the bed was not hard enough to begin with. But the board made the concrete hardness uniform instead of bumpy. I finally compromised on a few regular calisthenics in my cell. This proved to be more in keeping with my age and was proof against the weather, since the prison had no gymnasium for indoor sports.

Mental stagnation is not only bad in itself, but it can easily undermine physical health. Either you become conscious of this and combat it, or else you sink to one of the lower levels of prison existence. One of the most virulent forms of deterioration is brooding and self-pity. This is bad enough for the average prisoner, but for a political prisoner whom two justices of the Supreme Court—not to mention millions of other Americans—had held to be wrongfully jailed, the temptation to brood is strong indeed. The injustice of being in jail while crooks, thieves, warmakers, anti-Semites and lynchers roam the streets, is a difficult fact of life to adjust to. I never did succeed in wholly accomplishing serenity. Worst of all, to be barred from participation in the struggle for peace—the supreme issue of this mid-century—and for the liberation of the Negro and the colonial peoples, was the greatest threat to equilibrium.

On the other hand, there is the danger of a state of mind which regards everything that happens in prison as being of supreme importance. You seek to keep face within the community—a custom that flows naturally out of the isolated, stratified character of prison society. The least thing can be upsetting; pretty soon the environment of pettiness can become one's whole world. One has to learn to pick and choose what is of value and to avoid the "inner politics" of prison life. I sought to concentrate my main interest on those matters that were directly concerned with the real problems of society.

And, of course, it is not only the body but the mind which is imprisoned. The books, newspapers and periodicals I wanted to read and study were at the head of the *verboten* list: Marx, Lenin,

Stalin, Foster, the *Daily Worker*. Even though I was in prison and could "conspire" with no one, I was still not permitted to read Communist books. Unable to jail the books themselves, the government went to the worse outrage of putting the readers of such books in jail. But the library was jam-packed with the scribblings of Communist slanderers. There were two or three copies of Hitler's *Mein Kampf*.

Nevertheless, I found a certain value in acquiring some useful knowledge and in reading neglected books. The library did contain many valuable volumes—many of a classical character—which were not only worth reading but afforded opportunity for study and reflection—history, natural science, biography. My assignment to the library, which included handling books and manicuring the floor, greatly facilitated systematic reading, and I took full advantage of it.

An interesting irony is that Prosecutor McGohey had said during the trial that my "weapons were books," and that I now found myself assigned to handle more "weapons" in Terre Haute.

I was struck by the fact that once a dialectical outlook has been acquired, then such subjects as economics, natural science, history, and above all, mathematics (which may seem disconnected in bourgeois education), fall naturally into place. It will be a fine day for American kids when, under a socialist system, they learn that life is an integrated whole and that all studies are to enable man to be happier, to conquer life and nature.

Thus, reading became one of the most effective breaks in my prison routine. But I needed relief from that, too, if only to rest my eyes. For current literature, my friends on the outside sent me subscriptions to the *New York Times, Time* magazine and the Pittsburgh *Courier*—the largest of the Negro weeklies. This was the best my friends and I could do.

When I arrived at Terre Haute, the "velvet carpet," so to speak, had been prepared for me. Pictures of the jailed Communist leaders adorned every front page, headlines blinded the eyes, and radio commentators assaulted the ears. Seven of the Communist national board members were at last under lock and key—the country could breathe easier, although prices kept right on going up, the wages kept going down, and the lynch system continued to claim its black victims. Whatever people thought of our socialist convictions, even the most naive ought to have been able to see that we were not responsible for the ills actually afflicting them.

What the inmates at Terre Haute, and perhaps even some of the administration, who had never seen a Communist in the flesh, expected me to be like, I cannot imagine. From the flamboyant notoriety, was I expected to breathe fire and brimstone from my nostrils? I'm sure there were fears that I would "agitate" for my political views, and an agitator is just about the last thing any prison wants. If the government's publicity had grossly misrepresented my views, quite a few of the prisoners felt that they, too, had been misrepresented by the courts and that they shouldn't be here—that much, at least, we had in common.

Quite a few of the inmates were aggressively anti-Communist; sometimes from conviction; sometimes deliberately provocative. This hostility was manifested in jibes and sniping, and occasionally an attempt at missionary preaching to show me the error of my ways. Others went so far as to show me how lucky I was to be living in this great free country. And here we all were, in jail! A few of the inmates felt that they did not know enough about communism to be pro or con. Of course, I talked only to a comparative few; they could not resist the temptation to ask if what they read in the paper about me was true. And there was something in the paper almost daily.

In many instances, my sense of humor—which no one ever thought too much of—served me well. At some of the ridiculous jibes, I couldn't keep from laughing. They would seem more like slapstick comedy than serious questions. I could not undertake to answer all the innuendos and loaded questions. I did not have to be imprisoned to know that the life of a Communist in the United States was no bed of roses—being a Negro had left me no stranger to persecution.

Among the things I did to get away from the unpleasant facts of life in prison was my attempt to take one course at the prison school—Conversational Spanish, taught by one of the Latin American inmates. For a long time I had wanted to speak Spanish because of the large Spanish-speaking population in Harlem, with whom we Negroes had so much in common. I regretted that so few of our comrades had mastered the language. And I always envied William Foster who, though he had never had half as much formal education as I, spoke many languages and had a reading knowledge of still others. He always warned us about the tendency to think that only the citizens of the United States were Americans. His work, *Outline Political History of the Americas,* was a fundamental refutation of this kind of national chauvinism. He put great stock in the belief that it was part of the fight against chauvinist prejudices to learn the language of other peoples and converse with them in their own tongue. It's too bad I had to go to jail before I did much about it. (I'm sure the Department of Justice speculates that I'm taking Spanish so that I can escape abroad when I am released.)

If, as the federal system officials contend, the purpose of prison is to rehabilitate the prisoner, this is surely a long way from it. Just how was I to be rehabilitated? By being taught the virtues of capitalism, with the prison demonstrating such virtues so admirably? Can anyone with a straight face promulgate such virtues when capitalism is so bankrupt all over the world that Wall Street has to prop it up? It's capitalism that could do with a little rehabilitation—not I or my fellow Communist prisoners.

The fact that there is no special status for political prisoners in the United States is one more evidence of the backwardness of our social system. In Europe, even prior to World War II, such a status existed in many capitalist European countries. If the more enlightened penologists were inclined to grant a more humane status to political prisoners, the McCarrans and Joe McCarthys and other flag-wavers would hound them out of public life.

Neither I nor any other Communist chooses to be a martyr. We fought with all the resources at our command to prevent this government from doing such violence to traditional American liberties, to save the American working people from "thought control" persecution and from the catastrophe of another world war. That fight will go on no matter what happens to us as individuals.

Prison life is hard and stifling. All the while I am in jail, I cannot help thinking of my comrades who are being hounded and hunted as desperadoes—men of the finest mettle and devotion to the highest interests of the American people. The same Department of Justice that hounds them watches with silent acceptance while the big politicians raid the treasury of the United States, accept all manner of graft, head the biggest dope rackets, lynch Negroes and commit the most heinous crimes. Not only do these real criminals escape punishment, but often they are promoted to the highest office.

What was to be my attitude in jail—toward my fellow inmates and toward the prison officials? I had certain general ideas on the subject, but they were too sketchy to be useful. I had spoken to several of our comrades and other progressives who had "done time." But after a few weeks in Terre Haute, I discovered I had not talked enough. Our party people had always been too busy fighting for the other political prisoners—from Tom Mooney to the Scottsboro Boys—to give much consideration to how we ourselves would act as prisoners.

Toward the other inmates I felt that they, too, were victims of the prison system, as I was, and I expected them to look upon me in the same manner. On the whole, this is what happened—with some exceptions, of course. I soon learned that the primary thing on a prisoner's mind is the date of his release. And since this was my prime consideration, there was at least one preoccupation common to all of us.

Actually, most of my attitudes and views in prison had to be worked out as I went along. About many things I was inexcusably naive. It worked both ways: I was surprised at some of the things one could do, and even more amazed at some of the things one couldn't. An example of the latter was that if one lived in a cell block, one had to get an officer's permit to take a shower. Most of these surprises, however, were about the little things. And all the while one thing remained clearly etched in my mind—my class was the working class and it was the ruling class that had put me in jail.

Marx has said that a Communist must be interested in all the phenomena of life. If this is true for things, it is a million times more true for people. And in prison there are many, many types of people—from thwarted geniuses to inflated halfwits. It was interesting to observe and study some of them—evidently not an unusual pastime among prisoners. I was told once, for example, that I had been observed by one of the prisoners and that he had concluded that I was no Communist because I had a sense of humor. I replied, "Your idea of a Communist comes from the papers and the radio. Communists love life and specialize in good humor."

I learned, too, from the prisoners—sometimes unwittingly. Two or three of us drifted into a discussion of war one day, and they wanted to know my attitude. For about ten or 15 minutes I patiently explained my views, going into some detail. When I finished, rather pleased with myself, one of them asked bluntly: "Well, are you for or against war?" For a moment I was stunned. But the truth was that I had used such language, qualifications and fine shadings that only one as accustomed as I was to political discussion could possibly have understood me. I thought I was making myself clear, but I suspected that maybe my virtues as a popular speaker were somewhat overrated.

One gets news of all kinds in jail. Some of it has the impact of a bombshell. The news of Mother Bloor's death stunned me, although I knew that the last few of her 88 years had been very trying for her. Nevertheless, no one who had worked with her and learned to love and appreciate her could possibly be prepared for her death. She was one of the most truly great women this country has produced. She possessed a stout heart, an unquenchable fighting spirit, and a total devotion to the American working class and the poor farmers. Her love for people and for our party was as big as the seven seas. The mother of several children, some of them distinguished men and women, she nevertheless considered all of us as her sons and daughters and treated us that way. What a personification of the eternal youth of a fighting Communist! Her personality was always refreshing, her wit ready, her tongue sharp against the enemies of our party and the working class. I saw and heard her speak about a year and a half before her death, and even then her mind was as clear as a bell—in much better condition than her ailing body. Mother Bloor and her leadership were a living inspiration to millions of working Americans.

When I first became a member of the party, her words of encouragement had a great deal to do with my initiation into the spirit of brotherhood that prevails between Negro and white in the organization. Her sensitivity to the triple oppression of Negro women was boundless—I felt her loss as a deeply personal one.

When I had been in prison four months, my sister informed me of the death of my uncle, John Davis. I was saddened by this news, too, though I had not seen Uncle John in about 15 years and we had not been together very much since I was a boy in my early teens. But I remember him vividly. He had helped to rear my sister and me. He must have been in his late nineties at his death, and though wizened with age, he must have had a tough constitution—he never seemed to grow old. He was born in slavery, remembered his master, and used to relate the experiences of slavery and Reconstruction days to my sister and me. The older of my father's brothers, he was a carpenter and remained active at his trade until he was eighty. He wasn't particularly political-minded, but if he thought he had a point, he would stand his ground until the cows came home. One of the delights of my sister and me when we were kids, was to see Uncle John and our father get into a heated argument. My father, who had a brilliant mind and a fierce, indomitable will, would shout every argument under the sun at his brother and should have won by all the laws of logic and debate. But Uncle John would stick to his guns—never raising his voice and refusing to be intimidated. Often father would quit in sheer exasperation but Uncle John never quit. We admired father's brilliance, but our sympathies were with Uncle John. . . .

In addition to other diversions, I sought relief in the performance of normal prison duties. For example, our cells were subject to frequent official inspections. At such times one was required to have his cell in perfect order and cleanliness. This meant cleaning beds, bowls, sweeping, scouring, dusting and polishing everything within reach. Bon Ami and I struck up an acquaintance that was to find us inseparable throughout my term. I would apply myself with gusto to various tasks—anything to break the monotony.

But notwithstanding all the diversions and interests I could summon, nothing would relieve for long the natural oppressive atmosphere of prison, and the gnawing pain of being deprived of one's right to daily living and struggling. What I have written here with respect to my experiences in prison applies not only to Terre Haute but to the entire system, which I have evaluated, so far as I could, in the light of my Marxist outlook. I have given the reactions of a man unjustly in prison because of his political opinions. I agree with Mr. Justice Black and Mr. Justice Douglas that the imprisonment of me and my Communist colleagues under the Smith Act constitutes a monstrous violation of the Bill of Rights—particularly the First Amendment. In view of this, there is no jail that could be anything but hateful to me. I am not a criminal, not a menace to anyone. The real criminals, the real menace to the American people are the monopolies that are shoving our country down the road toward disaster, suffering, atomic war and fascism. As much as I value my freedom and resent being robbed of it, the crime against the peace and liberties of the American people is far more sinister.

Social revolutions are not made by Communists; they are made by capitalists who become so corrupt that they leave the people no basis for confidence in them, and the people have no recourse but to replace the system that breeds such suffering and privation. Communism is the science of replacing that system with a just and decent society.

APPENDIX

1. OF HYPOCRISY AND THE LIKE

A well-dressed and handsome Negro was making a religious talk to the student body at Morehouse College in the early 1920's. Members of the faculty sitting on the stage were giving him reverent attention. There was a hushed silence in the student audience. We had heard many such sermonettes—there was no time for a full sermon at the daily morning chapel service. Actually, we were fed up with these services because they so patently pandered to white Northern philanthropy. But we paid strict attention to this young speaker. His manner was the essence of sincerity and his message was delivered with culture and elegance.

He had been introduced by the most impressive of the faculty, Samuel ("Bigboy") Archer, a handsome six-footer of considerable prestige among the students. And his topic was a moral and religious indictment of hypocrisy. Knowing there was quite a bit of it in the college administration, we put our own interpretation upon his talk and listened with more than perfunctory interest.

The speaker was an ordained minister, a graduate of Shaw University in North Carolina and a YMCA secretary in Africa. This was my first acquaintance with Max Yergan.

Except for his subsequent visits to Morehouse, which I left in 1921, and for occasional articles in the papers about him, I lost track of Yergan for many years. He came into national prominence when he received the Spingarn Award of the NAACP for his missionary work in South Africa. I met him again in 1939 or the following year, when he became secretary of the newly established Council on African Affairs in New York City. It was founded by Yergan and Paul Robeson, largely with the latter's nest egg contribution. Robeson's deep interest in the struggle of Africans for liberation from colonialism had been kindled by a trip to Africa, where he saw at first hand the unbelievable brutality of imperialism. He also saw the connection between the plight of the American Negro and the African peoples. Still under the spell of Yergan's sermon at Morehouse many years ago, I felt that Yergan must have come to the conclusion that he was getting nowhere as a missionary financed by the same Rockefeller interests which kept colonials enslaved. Therefore, I thought, he had decided to shed that hypocrisy and to devote himself to African liberation. The Council was dedicated to freedom of the African peoples from imperialist domination and slavery.

Robeson's fame was already world-wide, and served as an excellent background for Yergan. Under these circumstances the contradictions within Yergan fully matured. He was still close to money, although not in the amounts that would have been accessible to him if he had continued with the Rockefeller-dominated General Education Board. But here he enjoyed another advantage, which was perhaps worth the sacrifice. He could now appear as an anti-imperialist radical, publicly championing the Africans, without sacrificing his luxurious mode of life. He could retain his comfortable middle class existence and exclusiveness while advocating the policies of anti-imperialism. He functioned as the chief executive officer of the Council, and no one knew better than he that the prestige of the Council rested on the integrity and leadership of Robeson, who enjoyed the full confidence of Negro and white forces in the labor and progressive movements which had a strong commitment to the African freedom struggle.

Somehow Yergan managed to avoid various pressures within the Council for concrete actions to implement its declared program. Actions such as research help, relief and financial aid to African freedom movements were undertaken by others. When occasionally Yergan found it impossible to avoid identifying himself with more militant mass activity, like the crusade against lynching in 1946, he would do so as an individual, without involving the Council or its supporters, for fear of antagonizing the well-off white élite whom he alone cultivated. He worked at this assiduously. He would leave the office, carrying his stylish portfolio, and return with a few hundred dollars after spending the afternoon with some wealthy scion—a typical Yergan "conquest."

In 1941, Yergan became president of the National Negro Congress. Under his magic touch, the Congress also became a "closed circle"—manipulated in his own cliquish style of work. The Congress had made history in organizing the unorganized, in building a solid membership among Negro workers, in helping establish the CIO and creating a pro-labor sentiment among Negro people. Such work had to be sustained primarily with the support of the masses that it engaged in struggle, but the hand-outs which Yergan got from his few white benefactors, while ignoring the pressure of the militants for mass action, were insufficient to keep the head of the Congress above water. Subsequently, it dissolved itself by the voluntary action of its frustrated members and supporters. Although this was not the only reason for the demise of the Congress, Yergan's role certainly hastened it.

The Communists were among the supporters of the Council on African Affairs. When, in 1945, they rejected the revisionist policies of Earl Browder, this was a shock to Yergan. He had been drawn to Browder's line of accommodation to capitalism, and he used his close personal association with Browder to his own advantage among Communists. At this point, Yergan did not know which way to turn, and for a moment he lost his bearings. When I met Yergan during the party's debate on Browderism, he was redder than the rose. He wanted to know why the entire party leadership had not resigned in a body, urging a drastic party purge of all who had even a speaking acquaintance with Browder. But this was merely Yergan's peculiar way of defending Browder, for he did not dare to defend him openly since it was clear that the party was going to reject him. At the same time, he feared that Browder would carry with him a significant number of middle class donors, upon whom Yergan depended. He decided to wait and see how the bourgeoisie was going to react to the change in the party. He had not too long to wait.

The witch-hunting drive in the interests of the Cold War soon came, and the Council was put on the Attorney-General's list of

Communist-front organizations. Yergan was now at the point where he had to choose. Without consulting his colleagues in the Council, he issued a press statement in the vein of the usual red-baiting slander against Communists. When this was rejected by the Council, he tried to wreck it by opposing "Communist domination," manipulating proxies, and appealing to the courts to sustain his claim that the Council's properties were his own. He went so far as to denounce Robeson as a "dupe of the Communists."

His actions become so revolting that even his closest middle class friends could no longer stomach him. Soon he slid to the very bottom, cooperating with the House Un-American Committee behind closed doors against his former friends and associates, many of whom suffered persecution as a result. As a reward, the State Department issued him a passport to go to Africa, and subsequently he was granted a visa by the Hitlerite Malan Government to enter South Africa. He became an apologist for Malan's racism and therefore it was no surprise when, in 1953, he praised President Eisenhower's appointment as U.S. Delegate to the United Nations of James Byrnes, the racist governor of South Carolina. Even many of his new-found friends, among them Walter White, denounced him. If the Cold War regime had intended to build Yergan into another Whittaker Chambers or—perhaps, more likely—into still another American Negro to be sent abroad as an apologist for racism in this country, his usefulness had evaporated.

It is somewhat academic to ask if Yergan were ever sincere. As Lenin once said, there is no such instrument as a "sincerometer" to measure an individual's honesty. It is now clear to me that he was not sincere even when he made that speech in Morehouse that so impressed me in my youth. All his life he merely sought gold for himself. Even as a missionary in Africa he lived in physical luxury. Just before he made his infamous choice he married a wealthy and attractive woman. He always took special care not to leave any written record of opinion or ideology which might later be used against him. He made only one unique contribution. In all my 20 years of participation in the Negro free-

dom movement I had never witnessed such a striking example
of political immorality and corruption in a middle class Negro
"leader." There have been many examples of Negro middle class
elements who have played constructive and useful roles, but
Yergan did demonstrate, as least as far as I am concerned, the
pitfalls of middle class leadership as such. I am confirmed in my
view that middle class individuals can play positive roles best
when they identify themselves honestly and completely with the
Negro working class, the true bearer of the banner of Negro
freedom.

2. THE DISTINCTION OF
BEING FIRST

Among certain upper circles of the Negro people it is considered a rare distinction to be "first"—the first Negro to be
appointed to this or that or to receive something not ordinarily
given to Negroes. Often a dubious distinction, it is in any case a
reflection of white supremacy society.

I do not take a negative view of appointment of Negroes to the
higher levels of government and private industry. It is a right
which has been consistently denied to the Negro, and should be
won. To do so in any meaningful way, even though such positions are held by a comparative few, the struggle has to be conducted against the national system of jim-crow and against its
benefactors, the wealthy ruling class. And when such a hill-top
position is won for a Negro here and there, the struggle does not
end. It must be continued against the very enemy class strong-
hold which had been forced to grant the position. For the class
enemy also tries to utilize the concession for its own ends, to
divert or abate continued struggle. Such concessions are forced—
not by the individual who gets the job but by the temper of the
Negro masses and their allies.

Many Negroes who have attained high posts make the mistake of thinking their own merit, education or culture secured them the job, although this is certainly a factor. Instead of using their positions to gain advantages for the mass of their people, they often go over to the ruling class or, at best, become indifferent to the Negro masses whose pressure put them there. If such individuals are to play a positive role they must remain loyal to the Negro masses in their struggle for freedom and full citizenship. If they go over to the ruling class they should be repudiated by the people.

To take an example: Billy Rowe, a columnist on the *Pittsburgh Courier,* has just (1951) been named a deputy police commissioner in New York City, thus becoming, *ipso facto,* a leader. This is the first time to my knowledge a Negro had been appointed to such a post, although as a sort of seventh assistant, assigned to "public relations"—a press agent for the police department. Two main reasons accounted for the appointment. First, the New York police department is widely hated in the Negro community for its unrestrained and murderous brutality. Commissioner Rowe's job will be to whitewash this record. Secondly, the widespread demand for a curb on police brutality forced the Mayor to make some sort of a concession. Actually, his appointment of Rowe served notice that nothing was to be done to curb police brutality, for Rowe was to function merely as an apologist. No wonder considerable public outcry was raised against this maneuver in Harlem.

One of the worst periods of police lawlessness against Negroes, trade unionists and Jewish and Puerto Rican groups in New York was in 1947, when Arthur Wallender was police commissioner. As a public service, I gathered statistics on the most violent cases and put them in a pamphlet, *Lynching—Northern Style.* The police department bought so many copies there was hardly any left for the people. Wallender was later forced to resign. After the wave of protests had receded, Mayor O'Dwyer appointed the anti-Negro Wallender head of the Mayor's Committee on Inter-racial Unity. Wallender conducted a campaign not against police brutality but against me for "calumny" of the police department. In view of the foul stench of corruption which later arose from that department it's hard to see how anyone could libel it.

Merely being a "first" is not sufficient to make a successful career. It's what you do as a "first," what you stand for, whose side you're on. Those "firsts" who take their stand with the class enemy are likely to have a successful career and a long life. On the other hand, if you're the first Negro to have the Supreme Court reverse a rape frame-up against you, then you're murdered in Eustis, Florida, for "attempting to escape"; if you are the first Negro to move out of a death-breeding slum into a more healthy environment like Cicero, Illinois, you risk being mobbed and your property destroyed, as happened to Harvey Clark. If you're the first to symbolize the sympathy of the Negro people for Communists by being elected a public official, you end up in Terre Haute penitentiary, where I am also the first Communist inmate.

The other kind of "firsts" I rarely considered a token of the "advancement of the Negro people." I don't see how those "first" worshippers who slavishly seek and obediently accept sell-out positions can expect to receive obeisance and homage from the Negro masses. They will be discarded by the ruling class as squeezed lemons when they are no longer able to bamboozle important sections of the Negro people. In the final reckoning, the Negro masses are bound to see through the opportunist game such individuals are playing, and will themselves discard them. Either way they cannot win.

3. A TRIP TO MEXICO

What is the mysterious concept of a "sinister and subversive" international conspiracy which was bandied about by Judge Medina and Prosecutor McGohey during the Foley Square trial? I can answer it quite simply: it is the association among workers and peoples of many lands, sharing their struggles, getting to know their customs and culture—whether in Asia, Europe, Africa, Latin America, or elsewhere. From the people in the colonial sections of the world, it can be learned how they are striving to throw off the yoke of exploitation and oppression and trying to establish people's democracies, socialism, self-determination—in other words, to become masters of their own destiny.

To be sure, one can study these phenomena from afar and understand them to some extent, but it is not the same as seeing them at first hand. Obviously, this kind of "international experience" is of inestimable value. It is too bad that more of our own people cannot get this invaluable international experience. For the most part it is still confined either to the rich who can afford travel, or to a handful of individuals in the labor and revolutionary movement who travel to represent their organizations. Americans ought to be allowed to discover that the United States is part of the world—and not the other way around.*

The nearest I came to international experience was the trip I made to Mexico in the first half of 1944. But my trip was really too short to fall into the category of international education. I stayed only a week, but it was a thrilling experience. I represented the National Committee of the Communist Party of the United States at the national convention of the Communist Party of Mexico, and I spoke at several sessions.

The opening session was held in an auditorium of a government building in Mexico City, and the public was invited. Fully four or five thousand people were present in the crowded auditorium. One of the high-ranking officials of the Mexican national

---

* A member of the House Un-American Committee once tried to bait me when I was testifying on behalf of my party: "Davis," he asked, "have you ever been to Rooshia?" "No," I replied, "I've never had the honor or the pleasure." Turning red in the face, he exclaimed: "What! That's an unpatriotic statement. You ought to be ashamed of yourself." So here I am sitting in my cell at Terra Haute still burning with the unpatriotic desire to visit "Rooshia," and not at all overcome with shame.

government spoke, testifying to the popularity and influence of
the party.

As spokesman of the American party, I received a tremendous
ovation. It was fully ten minutes before I could begin my speech
—which was translated by an interpreter. But there was so much
applause when the dramatic rendering of the interpreter was
relayed to the audience, that I was sure he was making a much
better speech to the audience than I had made to him. He ges-
ticulated, his voice rose and fell—how he got all that out of the
dry words I was nervously uttering, I never discovered. I knew
the content of my speech was not that spectacular and eloquent
in comparison with the heights of oratory that can be reached in
the beautiful Spanish tongue. Some of the speeches I heard in
Spanish were so expressive I could understand parts of them
without knowing the language.

Later I asked the general secretary to explain the audience
reaction, and he told me that the Mexican workers were exceedingly happy that the American party had sent a leading Negro
representative—one who had been elected to the New York city
council. The working-class Mexicans are in a sense an oppressed
people, and they could appreciate vividly the conditions of the
Negro in America. "Anyway, if your speech had not been good,"
he told me, "the interpreter would not have been able to do
much with it."

I could not spend much time in Mexico, for I could scarcely
afford to miss more than a week of the council sessions. The
Mexican party arranged a tour for me around the city, and I
witnessed the same contrasts I could see every day in New York—
except that the upper level in the United States was probably
higher than the corresponding level in Mexico, and the lower
level even lower. The streets in the main square of Mexico City
were clean and spacious. But ten blocks from there, where the
masses of workers lived, the squalor was unbelievable—hovels
flat on the ground, without running water or electricity, workers
going barefoot, children and old people in rags.

The Mexican party leaders lived in small shacks, like the rest of the workers, with only a bed, a couple of chairs, a few books and a table. They had only the barest necessities. They worked for the party often without wages—were frequently paid by eggs, an occasional chicken or small quantities of farm produce which party members who were peons had collected from other peons. Yet the spirit and morale were indomitable.

The most oppressed section of the Mexican population are the peons. Although I had no time to visit the agrarian area, the party leaders told me about conditions there at great length, and I followed the speeches of some of these comrades at the convention. Many are worse off than the sharecroppers and peons in the states of Mississippi, Georgia or Alabama.

Mexico is rich in natural resources, such as oil and silver. But these riches are drained off by Wall Street banks and industrialists. I recall the national humiliation to which Mexico was subjected by the government of the United States during my lifetime—once during Wilson's intervention against the Mexican revolution and once by Secretary of State Cordell Hull, who tried to stop the Mexican government from dealing with its oil properties as it saw fit. But these are only the dramatic instances. The more crushing humiliations are those suffered by the Mexican people—daily and unspectacularly the victims of the U.S. monopoly bandits. Only one president I know of had the courage of his convictions—Lincoln, when he condemned the Mexican war. Even under Franklin D. Roosevelt, the grip of Wall Street upon Mexico was tightened, not loosened. In February 1952 at Terre Haute I got a kick out of the news that the Mexican government refused to accept American domination under the guise of aid. That was a real slap in the face also to our former Mayor O'Dwyer, then Ambassador to Mexico.

This trip provided my first brush with the American political police. I had travelled by plane, and when I arrived in Corpus Christi, Texas, I was accosted by a government agent on the airfield. I showed him my credentials, including the introduction I had from the president of the city council, Newbold Morris. I happened also to have a couple of "police courtesy cards" issued to councilmen by New York's "finest." Finally, the agent was convinced that I was Benjamin J. Davis of New York. Nevertheless, he went over the contents of my bag with a fine-tooth comb. He went through my pockets and came across a few notes I had been making on the plane in preparation for my speech. When he found this scribbling—which I myself could barely decipher—he acted as if he'd found the *pièce de resistance,* in the form of direct orders from Stalin. He smacked his lips, left the room presumably to confer with someone else, returned and declared that I could proceed "but these writings will have to stay behind." I took this piece of rude political snooping in my stride. The notes and scraps were practically valueless—I made better notes on the flight to Mexico City. One more confiscation of my notes and I would have had a really first-rate speech. (I had practically forgotten those notes until, several months later, they were sent back to me at my office in New York. I'm sure the FBI made enough copies to use for throwaways. They were kept long enough for the whole personnel of the American thought-controllers to memorize them verbatim.)

In a few days my "international experience" was over. It had been a great privilege and honor to represent the American party. The contact, limited as it was, with the Mexican workers and progressives provided one of the great experiences of my life. I learned about other peoples in Latin America. I met representatives of several other Communist parties below the Rio Grande—a splendid group of people's leaders, some of them holding high elective office in their governments. One or two were senators. Thus, there was hardly any reason for the U.S. Communists to rest on their laurels. For the best our party had produced in the parliamentary field was a couple of city councilmen. We had a long way to go and I was keenly conscious of it.

Incidentally, the international trips of all of the 11 Communists were exhaustively gone into and batted about by the government prosecutors at Foley Square in 1949, the stage having been set for this by the lying testimony of government stoolpigeons. Some of these rats had gone so far as to imply that American Communists who had visited the Soviet Union had gone to learn to make bombs, to be taught the art of assassination, and so forth. As if these arts could not be learned in America, whose whole foreign policy is based upon the atom bomb. Indeed, there is no better place to learn of terrorist weapons than . America. I think of the Christmas Day (1951) assassination of Harry T. Moore and his wife, the countless bombings of Negro homes, Jewish synagogues and Catholic parishes from Illinois to Florida. . . .

I conclude by adding that I found the Mexican people a proud, dignified people, as much an integral part of the Western Hemisphere and so-called "Western civilization" as our own people. They are true Americans, but national chauvinism has misappropriated this name to apply only to the people of the United States. The civilization of Mexico is older and in many ways more beautiful than our own—we could afford to be more modest in our treatment of the Mexicans and all the people who live in Latin America.

4. A WEEK-END IN THE FAR WEST

The California party organizations had long wanted me to come to San Francisco and Los Angeles. I had visited nearly every other section of the country since my election to the city council. These were valuable trips; I always acquired new information, met other legislators with whom I exchanged legislative ideas. Most of these had followed my election campaign in New York and were anxious to learn at first-hand how it had been conducted. I found, too, that wherever I went the Negro people took great pride in my election, feeling encouraged by the fact that it was at last possible to break through the Republican-Democratic machines and elect independent spokesmen of their own.

It was late in January of 1946 when I set out for California. I arrived in San Francisco by plane and was immediately whisked away to a dizzying round of meetings, banquets, parties and conferences. In the two days and nights I spent in San Francisco, I must have attended ten affairs—culminating in a large public rally. In between, I was driven about on sightseeing tours. There was one hill overlooking the bay that was the most beautiful natural sight I'd ever seen. It looked like a painting—a composition of blues from the bay waters, greens from the grass-covered hillside, white-trimmed boats in the bay and a clear pastel-blue sky, forming a soft, transparent veil for the brilliance of the sun. The famed California weather was at its best. It was about 75 degrees and lovelier than the best spring day of May in Manhattan. I thought: What a beautiful country America is! And how befouled by exploitation and oppression! How wonderful it would be when the working class—the American people—took it over!

One of the most spirited and impressive sessions I had was with a large turnout of AFL and CIO unionists. I knew that the San Francisco workers were a real vanguard among trade unionists, having produced such a great labor leader as Harry Bridges. I learned much more from these workers than they did from me, since one of the blank areas in my background was the absence of substantial and individual trade union experience.

In addition, I met the leaders of the Negro community—lawyers, doctors, political, labor and church leaders. I spent many pleasant and fruitful moments with them, comparing notes on our respective communities. I found out that the Negro trade unionists were not only the most militant leaders of their people —they were also the physical links between the Negro community and the organized labor movement. They were a fine lot and helped to give one confidence in the eventual liberation of the working class and of the Negro.

My next stop was Los Angeles, and there was the same round of meetings, conferences and receptions. I spoke at a very large Negro church; this was later followed by a meeting attended by some 4,000 people—fully a third Negro. I was surprised to find so many Negroes who had known my father or my family or even myself as a boy. And it was in Los Angeles that I met the distinguished Negro leader, Mrs. Charlotta Bass. She was as well known in the East as she was on the West Coast, as editor and publisher of the *California Eagle,* as a militant spokesman for Negro rights and a close and loyal supporter of the labor movement. Her paper was an institution in Los Angeles and it possessed influence far beyond its relatively small circulation. The *Eagle* was the voice of the Negro masses and was incorruptible.

Mrs. Bass was exceedingly able and intelligent, looking upon the struggles of the Negro people in terms of the entire global picture. The loss of her young nephew in World War II (he had been a columnist on her paper and was very close and dear to her) was a powerful blow. But she decided she would have to become far more active in the peace movement so that other beloved nephews would not have to die.

I was not at all surprised when, in March of 1952, I read that she was to be the vice-presidential candidate of the Progressive Party in the national elections. Her nomination in itself made history, since it was the first time in American political history that a Negro woman had been nominated for so high an office.

Mrs. Bass and I had a long discussion while I was in Los Angeles, and every moment of it was precious to me. With her rich discernment and wisdom, she also had a warm, maternal heart that could comfort people and put them at their ease. . . .

I was told by a group of party leaders that a very important appointment had been arranged for me. We went downtown to the business section where, in a large building, I met a group of public officials. The man who met me at the door was a member of the Seattle city council, who introduced me to six other members of the council. They had called a special informal session to greet me and to discuss the municipal affairs of our respective cities. I was overwhelmed. Pictures were taken; there were interviews with the press. None of the councilmen were even left-wingers and there were no labor or Negro or Communist members. I found a way to suggest that in the latter respect the New York situation was more advanced than theirs. It was altogether a pleasant surprise that my comrades had arranged.

Late that afternoon I was scheduled to fly back to New York. I already had my plane ticket but I dreaded the trip. My experience from Los Angeles to Seattle had not filled me with any zest for another long, unpredictable plane ride. And I was exhausted from the terrific pace of my schedule on the West Coast. On the plane I'd be back in New York overnight and would have to plunge directly into council work. So I decided to go by train. This would give me three days of relaxation, a breathing spell, and enable me to see the country as well. I cancelled my plane reservation and boarded the train. I slept with the soundness of complete exhaustion and arose the next morning fresh and very hungry.

When I went to the dining car, the steward gave me a morning newspaper. I almost jumped out of my seat when I read the headline: "Plane crashes—19 killed. No survivors. Five-thirty airliner bound for New York from Seattle smashes head-on into the mountain side."

I pretty nearly lost my appetite. That was a close call, too close for comfort. I told the waiter about it, but since he had recognized me, he was far more interested in two other matters: Did I know Paul Robeson? And what was a Communist? We became buddies on the way to Chicago, where I changed trains.

Suddenly it dawned upon me that my plane reservations had been made in New York before I left. My comrades knew I was scheduled to be on that plane. I could imagine the fears of the people back home. I sent a telegram to the party center—but it was delayed. When I got back I learned that for a while the whole national office had been checking, expecting the worst. Someone, however, called the state party headquarters in Washington and learned that I had taken the train.

When I got to Chicago, something else that was unscheduled happened.

I was sitting in the railroad station, waiting for my train connection, when I was hailed by a Negro man who carried a small bag with his Pullman porter's cap attached to it. "Aren't you Ben Davis?" he asked.

Then he identified himself. He had an aunt who was very

active in the Harlem Communist Party. He had heard her speak of me quite often. He was happy to meet me. I asked him where he was going, and he said to New York.

"I'm on my way to New York, too," I said happily, certain I was going to have a friend all the way home.

"That's too bad," he said. "I'm a porter on the 20th Century Limited. I'm going now to make my run."

I thought for a moment; then I said, "Let me go with you."

"Are you kidding? That train's booked weeks ahead. Besides, it's hard for Negroes to get reservations. You have no ticket and you can't get one. Wish I could help you. I'd sure like to have you along."

"You can get me on somehow."

"But, Mr. Davis, you're a councilman, a leader of our people. You can't do that."

"That's what I want to do, especially. Will you get me on and make up a good story? Just don't tell the conductor—under any circumstances—who I am."

He agreed. I got on with him. After the train started, the crisis came quickly. The conductor spied me, and although I stuck close to my porter friend, he demanded my ticket and reservations. I started to explain, hoping my friend would rise to the occasion. He did, magnificently.

He told the conductor a story that almost had me weeping. I was a lifelong family friend who had to get to New York before my mother died. But the conductor wasn't that easily convinced and he threatened to stop the train at the Englewood Station to put me off. My porter friend talked up a breeze, any minute on the verge of divulging my identity, but I kept my hand on his coattail to remind him of his bargain.

Finally the conductor relented with a sharp warning to my friend. I was afraid that I had jeopardized his job, but he reassured me that things like this often happened with members of porter's families and that the conductor was a "good guy." I was at ease.

Another Negro could be squeezed on the super-de-luxe Twentieth Century but not as a passenger, only as a servant. I ate and slept as a porter all the way to New York. What I didn't learn first-hand about the life of the porters wasn't worth listening to! These fellows are treated subhumanly by the Pullman Company. What it does to their bodies is enough, but what it does to their dignity is even worse.

When I finally arrived in New York from my luxurious and incognito Twentieth-Century ride, I passed the conductor. I told him who I was, and he said: "And I'm Mayor O'Dwyer." I kept on walking and looking back and saw one of the porters telling him something. The conductor watched me and scratched his head.

5. ANYTHING CAN HAPPEN

I had always thought—perhaps presumptuously—that I was pretty well known, certainly to the omniscient federal government. In any case, my name was widely known among the Negro people, largely because of my father's prominence in the fraternal, political and journalistic fields.

True, in my late twenties and early thirties, I had been confused on several occasions with B. O. Davis, Jr., son of the sole U.S. Negro general during World War II. When B. O. Davis, Jr. was appointed to West Point, I received several messages of congratulations meant for him. (I wondered subsequently if he received similar felicitations when I was elected to the city council. If I ever meet "B.O.," I intend to ask him that question.)

I had been known among the older generation of Negroes as the "son of Ben Davis." I can thank American reaction in no small measure for helping to carve out an individual niche for me. First, it was its electoral corruption in New York that stirred the people to elect me to public office. Then I got sent off to prison with a five-year sentence that gave me a further identifying mark.

In 1939 my individual credentials were not so well known, and the FBI was somewhat at sea. It was the period when the Soviet Union had signed a non-aggression pact with Nazi Germany. The reactionaries proceeded to condemn and persecute everyone who saw the pact as the result of the collapse of Soviet appeals for collective security, as a self-defense move on its part to checkmate, if possible, the attempt of Chamberlain, Daladier and similar forces in the United States to drive Hitler to the East.

Immediately after the pact, the well-known hysteria machine of American reaction began its red-baiting worst. In little or no time the atmosphere of the country had changed, white became black, everything was turned upside down; fear and hysteria ruled. Never had the monopolists turned their wrath on Hitler as they now did against the Soviet Union. The Bill of Rights was fast becoming a scrap of paper.

I was then on the editorial board of the *Daily Worker*. It became necessary to defend the free speech rights of the paper. Title to the paper was transferred to three women with distinguished careers as partisans of civil liberties. An administrative and editorial group was selected (of which I was one) to guarantee the continuity of the paper's policy.

The change had barely been made in time. The officers of the paper were hailed before a grand jury in Washington. The crime of which the *Daily Worker* was accused was that it had opposed the Munich Pact of 1938 and upheld the Soviet-German Non-Aggression Pact of 1939. The persecution proceeded under the guise of investigating whether the *Daily Worker* was a foreign agent—ruled by Moscow, of course—and if so, it was guilty of having refused to register as a foreign agent.

It was a witch-hunt, a fishing expedition, in the name of national security. I had never before appeared before a grand jury; this was to be my first experience in a star-chamber proceeding.

I did have a touch of stage fright when I was called into the jury room, but my mind was clear. When I looked around, I saw two Negroes sitting at the back of the room by themselves. Members of the grand jury, they were segregated—in the true "capital of democracy" style—even in the jury room. This added fuel to the flames of anger and resentment already burning within me.

I took a seat at the witness table in front of the jurors.

"What is your name," an officious young attorney asked.

"Benjamin J. Davis," I answered.

"Are you sure?" he inquired.

"Quite," I said.

"You're not Benjamin F. Davis, whose home is in Trinidad, and who came to this country when he was nine years old, are you?" he asked.

"Of course not. What are you driving at?"

"I'll ask the questions," he stated.

"Are you then the Davis who immigrated from Jamaica several years ago?"

"No," I said impatiently.

"Are you quite sure you're not in the country illegally?" he persisted.

I looked straight at him. "I was born in Dawson, Georgia. Draw your own conclusions."

Some of the jurors snickered.

This attorney was bent on proving me an alien; he was depriving me of my citizenship by utterly nonsensical questions. He wanted to plant in the minds of the jurors that all Communists are foreigners. It was the first time my citizenship had been challenged. In the midst of a wave of hysteria, all things are possible.

The remainder of my questioning was brief. The young bloodhound was quite hotheaded. But he had made the mistake of sniffing at the wrong scent.

"Your job on the *Daily Worker* is to carry out the anti-American policy of Moscow, isn't it?" he asked triumphantly.

"My job is to work in the interests of democracy and peace, and to oppose jim-crow and lynch law against Negroes."

He flushed, but continued: "There are laws in this country against those things and the government is supposed to enforce them—isn't that so?"

"Yes, there are some good laws, but they're not enforced—for example, the 13th, 14th and 15th Amendments. The Congress has refused to pass an anti-lynch law, and they don't seem interested in investigating lynching."

By this time he was noticeably angry and he lost his head. "You've never been discriminated against in this country. You've gone to the best schools. What do you mean saying there's discrimination in Washington?" he bellowed.

"Well, if you must know, there was discrimination in the schools I attended. As for Washington, it's the worst jim-crow city in the country. When I leave this room, I can't go to a place to eat downtown. I can't get hotel accommodations, I can't go to a theatre. Where've you been? I'll inform you that it's a humiliating experience to be a Negro in Washington. You're investigating me—but doing nothing about those who violate my constitutional rights."

He said nothing. He was out of his depth.

The two Negroes in the back of the room, rather listless up to now, sat erect in their chairs. They knew from their own humiliations that I spoke the truth. They seemed glad it was spoken, even if they could not applaud me.

After the exchange between the young prosecutor and myself, the questioning was abruptly ended and I was dismissed.

Bob Minor, editor of the *Daily Worker,* had also been called into the chamber, and he almost evoked applause from the jury. This was indeed an inexperienced prosecutor, and his inquisition was boomeranging.

The pseudonyms used by two or three of the *Daily Worker* officials, which were later adduced as sinister proof of Communist conspiracy during the Smith Act prosecutions, didn't upset the Department of Justice much. They only required that real names be published at the masthead of the paper. We agreed to the stipulation and the inquisition was dropped. And, incidentally, I regained my citizenship, which I was perilously close to losing in the anti-Soviet hysteria. As I think about it, if the inquisition had continued, I might have ended up being born in Soviet Georgia and conveniently smuggled into Georgia, U.S., during my infancy to help make the Communist revolution. Anything can happen.